Mandate for
21st Century America:
Universal Health
Insurance

David F. Drake

PublishAmerica
Baltimore

First printing

ISBN: 1-4241-6546-6
PUBLISHED BY PUBLISHAMERICA, LLLP
www.publishamerica.com
Baltimore

Printed in the United States of America

Table of Contents

List of Tables

What Reviewers Said About
Mandate for 21ˢᵗ Century:
Universal Health Insurance

Jeff C. Goldsmith
President, Health Futures, Inc.

"As health reform rises yet again to the top of the domestic policy agenda, David Drake's *Mandate for 21ˢᵗ Century America* stakes out a sensible middle ground in a perpetually gridlocked ideological debate. A health policy veteran, Drake argues for tax-financed universal coverage based on private markets, an achievable policy leaves consumers exposed to first dollar costs and providers accountable for their costs. As the costs and consequences of doing nothing becomes indefensible, Drake's 'third way' approach will become increasingly attractive to pragmatic policymakers. It is well worth reading."

Kenneth E. Raske
President & CEO
Greater New York Hospital Association

"Mandate for 21ˢᵗ Century American should be required reading for all Presidential hopefuls in the '08 election. There has not been a serious healthcare policy debate since the Clinton plan in 1993-1994. We are way overdue in tackling tough issues in healthcare."

Stephen Shortell
Dean of School of Public Health
And Blue Cross of California Distinguished
Professor of Health Policy and Management
University of California, Berkeley

"If the time has come for comprehensive healthcare reform, David Drake's *Mandate for 21ˢᵗ Century Americans: Universal Health Insurance* provides the direction for how to get it accomplished. Insightful and well-argued, it should be read by all who engage this uniquely American challenge."

Preface

Writing this book at this time was inspired by the financial difficulties of the American automobile industry, specifically the problems Ford and General Motors are experiencing primarily because of generous employee benefits in their labor contracts. A subsequent event, the Massachusetts miracle in passing universal health insurance legislation, did not figure into the timing at all, but that is a quite remarkable story, both for its bipartisan agreement between a Republican governor and a Democrat-controlled legislature and an innovative means of financing health insurance for 99 percent of Massachusetts residents. The auto industry story has much more significance for federal health insurance legislation.

For generations, the auto workers' health benefit had been the Cadillac (coincidental pun) of health insurance policies—extremely comprehensive coverage with minimal deductibles and copayments—and one of the proudest accomplishments of the United Auto Workers for its members. Last December, a bare 51 percent of Ford's union members voted to approve cutting more than 18 percent of their health insurance benefits in a concession for the financial well being of their company, a day after a U.S. District Court granted approval to a similar concession at GM. Although I had observed over the past several years that more employers were pushing more health premium costs onto workers and an increasing number were taking the drastic step of eliminating the health insurance benefit altogether, the changing of the UAW contract on health benefits was similar in magnitude in the health insurance business to the fall of the Berlin Wall in international politics. For decades the auto health insurance benefit set the standard that all unions (and most Americans) aspired to obtain as an employee benefit. Health insurance is no longer affordable because health care is no longer affordable.

The world has changed. As I began to consider its implications, I was immediately struck by how this diminution in employee benefits would affect the legislative consideration of federal health insurance, a subject that has long interested me. After retiring from the American Hospital Association, I wrote a book, *Reforming the Health Care Market: An Interpretive Economic History*, that was published by Georgetown University in the fall of 1994 just after the Clinton health reform plan had been shot down in Congress. At that time, a myth was created that said the United States would never enact federal health insurance—it was too big a step for such a conservative nation; health care reform would have to be enacted incrementally. Alas, my own studies convinced me that the problems with the American health care system are systemic and cannot be reformed incrementally. The legislative history of health insurance in the United States suggests that federal health insurance will never be enacted in this country as long as most middle class Americans remain satisfied with the health insurance provided by their employers—tax free—as a benefit. However, the auto industry news last December could well be a precursor of the first major breakdown in the sixty-year history of employee health insurance. As that breakdown continues and spreads, federal health insurance will gain political viability and legislative consideration.

I also realized that there is a very strong reason to expect more employers to consider reducing or capping their health insurance liability. That reason is globalization of trade. The peculiar way that Americans chose for, or more accurately fell into the practice of, financing health care at the place of employment puts American companies at a competitive disadvantage in world labor markets. All other developed nations chose to finance health care through various national health insurance programs, which made business one of several payers for the insurance system in contrast to the American approach that made business the principal purchaser for American workers. I think that it's a fairly safe prediction that more businesses will try to restructure their employee health insurance benefit and only slightly riskier to forecast the business sector, as a political entity, will soon be campaigning for federal health insurance as a means of capping its liability. Business's unwillingness to continue bankrolling employee health insurance will also be the Achilles heel in the Massachusetts health plan.

Business support for federal health insurance will surely cause a revolution in the Republican Party, leading to the support of federal health insurance by many of the Republican candidates for president in 2008. That election could well become the nation's first federal health insurance election, with both presidential candidates supporting their parties' vision for health care reform in the United States and the 111th Congress, convening in 2009, could be the one to finally enact federal health insurance. If so, the Massachusetts political experience is vital, for it will take a bipartisan effort to enact federal health insurance. In that respect, the Massachusetts' legislative triumph may yet have real political significance.

My prior experience of publishing a book on health care reform just after one of the most cataclysmic legislative defeats in America's health care reform history led me to the conclusion that I had best start writing immediately. This time I hope to lead, rather than follow, the legislative history of health care reform in the United States. I may still be ahead of the health insurance legislative curve and this time I hope to contribute to that dialogue.

If I can, it's because friends agreed to review and comment on my manuscript. The one problem of writing in retirement is the lack of colleagues to inspire or deter that I had at AHA or the University of Chicago where I taught for many years. These friends include Tom Galinski, Bob Hepple, Perry Johnston, Dave Oatway, and Sam Williams and my son Andrew, all of whom have stuck through the whole process, providing me with encouragement through comments and suggestions and a bit of discouragement when I got carried away. Their efforts are greatly appreciated, but the responsibility for errors is solely mine.

Finally, nothing I do would be possible without the wholehearted support of my wife, Joyce. She has not only reviewed every draft of this manuscript, making many helpful suggestions, but even more important, always giving me encouragement and inspiration. As much as she deserves the book's dedication, I must dedicate it to her only prior claimant for my esteem, my older brother who died earlier this year after serving as my mentor for nearly seventy years.

David F. Drake
Beverly Shores, Indiana
November 2006

DEDICATION

To Robert Edwin Drake

October 11, 1923 to January 12, 2006

In loving memory and appreciation

CHAPTER 1
The Broken U.S.
Health Care System

As we enter the 21ˢᵗ century, the American health care system is badly broken. And it's getting worse all the time. The U.S. health care system is the highest cost health system in the world; it provides the lowest level of access to care for all its citizens of any developed nation in the world; and, it even puts its patients at greater risk of safety infractions than most other developed nations. In a single word, the American health care system is broken and needs to be fixed. In this chapter, we will first document these three charges of higher cost, lower accessibility, and poorer patient safety in the American health care system. After outlining the many, failed reform attempts in the previous century, we consider why this first decade in the 21ˢᵗ century may be the time for the United States to finally enact a national health insurance program to reform its broken system. And third, we outline the reasons America's broken health care system must be replaced, not simply incrementally reformed over time, which has been the American political tradition. The chapter concludes by summarizing the content of the remainder of the book.

THE DISMAL RECORD OF THE
AMERICAN HEALTH CARE SYSTEM

Higher Costs in the American Health Care System

The United States, together with 29 other developed nations, is part of the Organization for Economic Cooperation and Development (OECD) that shares "a commitment to democratic government and the market economy." One of the principal activities of OECD is to assist these 30 countries in sharing data on the operation of their economies. The OECD data on health care costs may be employed to document the fact that the U. S. health care system is the highest cost of any nation in the developed world. Table 1.1 summarizes health spending in six representative developed nations since 1960 by reporting per capita health costs, adjusted for purchasing power disparities in currencies among these nations, and the percentage of the six nations' gross domestic product (GDP, the measure of total output of goods and services for domestic consumption) that is devoted to personal health care spending—spending on hospitals, physician and other professional services, dental services, home health and nursing home services, and drugs and medical equipment.

TABLE 1.1
Health Care Spending in Six Developed Nations for
Selected Years, 1960-2002 in Constant 2002 Dollars

Country	Health Spending Per-Capita 1960	1990	2002	Spending as percent of GDP 1960	1990	2002	Health Spending Chg Vis-à-vis GDP Chg
Canada	$662	$2,335	$2,931	5.4%	9.2%	9.6%	1.78
France	437	2,120	2,736	4.2	8.9	9.7	2.31
Germany	546	2,207	2,817	4.8	8.7	10.9	2.27
Japan	158	1,490	2,077	3.0	6.1	7.8	2.60
U.K.	449	1,315	2,160	3.9	6.0	7.7	1.97
U.S.	905	3,854	5,267	5.2	12.6	14.6	2.81

Source: Organization for Economic Cooperation and Development, OECD Health Data.

The table documents that in 1960 when data on health care was first collected by the OECD the United States spent 36.7 percent more than the second highest expenditure nation, Canada. That it spent 65.1 percent more in 1990 and that the disparity in spending had reached nearly 80 percent more than Canada in 2002. This increasing differential in spending suggests that throughout this entire 42 year period, health care spending in the United States has been rising faster than in Canada, which among these six nations has consistently spent more than any of these nations other than the United States.

In terms of how much a nation spends on health care of its total spending, the United States also leads the developed world by a considerable margin. Although Canada spent a higher portion of its total GDP on health care than the United States in 1960, 5.4 percent to 5.2, Canada's health spending grew at a slower rate relative to GDP growth than any of these six nations over these 42 years, only 1.78 times GDP growth (the last column). The United States in 2002 leads the world in the percentage of its resources devoted to health care spending, and it also had the highest multiple to GDP growth of 2.81, which means that health care spending is growing nearly three times faster than growth in its total GDP. Americans spend more of their resources on health care than any other nation in world and their spending has continued to grow faster than any nation over this entire 42 year period. America had a bad record of high costs in 1960 and it has gotten worse over the past four decades.

Since the United States spends so much more than any other nation on health care, one can ask the question: what additional health care services account for this quite significant difference in spending? Table 1.2 compares the number of medical services that the population of these six nations received in 2000. America provided fewer doctor visits to patients than any other country except the United Kingdom; it provided fewer hospital admissions than any country except Canada; it makes available fewer CT scanners than Germany or Japan; but it does provide the most coronary angioplasties per capita of any country in the world, by a wide margin (the second most active nation is Belgium with 201.4 per 100,000 population). Indeed, it also provides the third most renal dialysis per 100,000 population at 86.5, while Japan provides 162.4 and Poland provides 128.9, according to OECD reports.

TABLE 1.2
Health Care Utilization Statistics
In Six Developed Nations for 2000

Country	No. of Physician Visits Per Capita	Hospital Admissions Per 1000 Population	CT Scanners Per Million Pop.	Coronary Angioplasties Per 100,000 Population*
Canada	6.4	99	8.2	80.8
France	6.5*	204	9.6	N.A.
Germany	6.5*	205	17.1	165.7
Japan	16.5*	N.A.	84.4	N.A.
U.K.	5.4	151	6.5	51.0
U.S.	5.8	125	13.6	388.1

Source: Organization for Economic Cooperation and Development, OECD Health Data.
*Most recent data.

If Americans don't receive more bread and butter medical services, like doctor and hospital visits, why do Americans spend so much more on health care? Gerard Anderson [2003] and his colleagues concluded in a recent analysis of international health care systems that Americans, for various reasons, pay higher prices for virtually all medical care services; we shall want to return to this finding and examine some of the more important reasons for Americans paying higher prices for health care (see pages 26-38). As we shall also see, a second and related reason is that American physicians practice the most technologically intensive form of patient care in the world without any apparent improvement in patent morbidity or mortality.

Less Access to Care in the American Health Care System

In 2006, the United States is one of the only two developed nations (the other being the Union of South Africa) that does not have a national health insurance program, financed in whole or in part by government, to ensure that all people have equal access to health services. Instead the United States has a fragmented system of financing health care in which the federal government finances health

insurance for all persons 65 years of age and older through the
Medicare program (with some seniors acquiring supplemental
coverage from private health insurers paid for either directly or by
previous employers), a matching federal-state government program,
Medicaid, for lower income Americans regardless of age, and private
health insurance that is financed by employers and/or direct personal
payment. The remainder of the population is uninsured for health
services and is billed directly by health care providers for health services.

Table 1.3 summarizes the health insurance coverage Americans
have had over the past 14 years, by number of persons and percentage
of the population age group. First, the table's organization reflects the
complexity of health insurance financing in the United States. The
financing of Americans' health care is categorized into age,
employment, and income levels to sort out which coverage goes to
which individuals. Second, over this particular 14-year period health
insurance coverage is diminishing as fewer seniors are purchasing
supplemental coverage—more than 90 percent of seniors in 1989 had
additional coverage to supplement their Medicare coverage, while in

TABLE 1.3
American Health Insurance Coverage
For Various Years in Millions and in Percent of Age Category

Type of Coverage	1989		2000		2003	
Medicare	29.3	100.0%	33.4	100.0%	34.3	100.0%
Private Supplement	22.4	76.5%	21.2	63.4%	21.5	62.7%
Medicaid	2.0	15.2%	2.5	7.5%	2.7	8.0%
Medicaid (under 65)	15.4	7.2%	23.2	9.5%	30.9	12.3%
Private Insurance (under 65)	162.7	75.9%	174.0	71.5%	173.6	68.9%
Through Employment	146.3	68.3%	162.5	66.7%	159.3	63.3%
Direct Purchase	16.4	7.6%	11.5	4.8%	14.3	5.6%
None—Uninsured	33.4	15.6%	41.4	17.0%	41.6	16.5%
Persons, Under 65	214.0	87.8%	238.6	87.6%	246.1	87.8%
Persons, 65 and Over	29.3	12.2%	33.4	12.3%	34.3	12.2%
Total Population	243.3	100.0%	272.0	100.0%	280.4	100.0%

Source: U.S. Department of Health and Human Services, *Health, United States, 2005,*
Washington, DC: Superintendent of Documents, 2005, pp. 379-388.

2003, supplemental coverage had dropped to 70 percent—and as fewer of the employed have their insurance purchased through their employer—employer-purchased group health insurance (regardless of how the payment is split between employee and employer) is broader coverage than individually purchased coverage. The only real increase in insurance coverage during this period has been the increased participation in Medicaid by both over and under 65 year olds, more people are qualifying for low income government subsidies, still reflecting the downturn in the business cycle between 2000 and 2003.

The difficulty in accessing health care in the United States is concentrated on the more than 40 million Americans under 65 earning lower incomes (90 percent earn less than 200 percent of the poverty level income), but unable to qualify for Medicaid. Nevertheless, more than 60 percent of the uninsured are working [Lillie-Blanton and Hoffman], but their earnings are not sufficient to purchase health insurance. This group is disproportionately represented by minorities, with only about 16 percent of the white population (the lowest of any racial group) being represented while nearly 35 percent of the Hispanic or Latino populations are uninsured [USDHHS]. Uninsured persons are more reluctant to seek health care and when entering the health care system, they are more likely to receive inferior care [Burnstein, et al]

Most Americans are quite healthy, have few illnesses over their lifetimes, and have relatively low total health care costs over their entire lives [Roos et al]. Only a small portion of the total population have a significant amount of illness and incur substantial health care costs, and less than 10 percent have very serious health problems and will experience extraordinary health care costs during their lives. Berk and Monheit [2001] have summarized data on the distribution of health expenditures for the U.S. population for selected years from 1928 to 1996. Since 1970 five percent of the population in any given year has consumed more than half of all the nation's personal health care expenditures, and 30 percent has made about 90 percent of all expenditures. The insurance term, "adverse selection," refers to the fact that persons with the higher level of health care illnesses are more likely to purchase health insurance than healthier individuals. During these acute episodes of illness, low income Americans can qualify for government assistance through Medicaid, but logic suggests that these episodes are made more expensive and that lower income Americans suffer more severe illness by deferring care prior to becoming eligible for Medicaid. America's system of financing health care is inequitable, and the system's efficiency is not enhanced by this fragmentation and inequity.

Because of government income tax rules, the inequity also extends to the more than 60 percent of the population that has health insurance coverage. Those employed who obtain health insurance through their employers receive these benefits without having to pay income taxes on the value of the insurance. Others, who pay for their own health insurance through direct payment to insurance carriers, must purchase their insurance with after tax dollars; i.e., they receive no tax benefit from having health insurance. As the number of employers paying none or smaller portions of the insurance premiums continues to increase and the benefit of the current tax law is concentrated on a smaller segment of the work force, pressures will mount to amend the tax code and eliminate the tax exempt status of employer-paid health insurance premiums or provide an insurance tax subsidy for all purchasers of health insurance. Employer-paid health insurance is also under attack through global market competition because American employers are increasingly brought into competition with foreign enterprises that do not have health insurance premiums in their employee cost structure because their employees are insured through government programs. Not only are American firms at a competitive disadvantage because of the employer-financed system that Americans used to finance, but that disadvantage is magnified by the higher health costs in the United States. Businesses are likely to become the biggest boosters for health care reform in the United States in the near future.

Poorer Patient Safety in the American Health Care System
Americans are not only subjected to higher prices for medical care services financed in an inequitable manner, subjecting many lower income Americans to less and poorer care, but Americans are also put

at greater risk of error during their patient involvement with the American health system. Evaluating patient risk through cross-national comparisons of care in different health care systems is a relatively new form of research, but it is of increasing interest.

On one recent study, Cathy Schoen [2005] led a team of seven researchers primarily from the Commonwealth Fund that conducted a survey of sicker adults in six countries—Australia, Canada, Germany, New Zealand, the United Kingdom, and the United States—to determine the degree of safety risks, care coordination problems, and other general deficiencies in patient care in these countries. The countries were selected to study distinct insurance and health care delivery arrangements and sicker adults were chosen as the study subjects because they have the most experience with the health systems and are the group, as we saw in the last section, that incurs the bulk of the costs for care. The study found overall that: "The United States often stands out with high medical errors and inefficient care and has the worst performance for access/cost barriers and financial barriers" [Schoen et al]. Here are some of the categories in which the American system either led or had the second highest percentage of patient complaints:

1. American hospital staff only sometimes, rarely, or never did everything they could to control pain.
2. During a hospital stay, American patients were more likely to experience a communication failure in information sharing among care givers to the patient.
3. At discharge from the hospital, American patients were less likely to have someone discuss new drug prescriptions with them.
4. In the American patient's treatment a medical mistake was more likely to be made.
5. The American patient was more likely to be given the wrong medication or wrong dose.
6. The medication errors were less likely to be revealed to the American patients by their physicians.
7. American patients were more likely to be given the incorrect results of a diagnostic or lab test.

8. American patients experienced longer delays in being notified about abnormal test results.
9. American patients reported the highest number of medical, medication, or lab errors and experienced these errors while being treated by the largest number of physicians.
10. American patients take four or more medications for chronic conditions.
11. American patients only sometimes, rarely, or never received explanations about the side effects of the drugs they are taking.
12. American patients with diabetes were least likely to have annual eye examinations routinely made.
13. American patients suffering from chronic diseases were least likely to have regular physician care and to have had the same physician for 5 years or more.
14. American patients suffering from chronic diseases were the second least likely to have physicians make clear specific goals for care or treatment and to be told about treatment choices or options.
15. American patients suffering from chronic diseases most frequently complained about records or test results not reaching a doctor's office in time for their appointment.
16. American patients suffering from chronic diseases most frequently complained about coordination problems when they were treated by four or more doctors.
17. American patients had the greatest difficulty in obtaining physician treatment at night or on weekends and holidays and were the second most frequent visitors of emergency rooms.
18. American patients were less likely, by a quite sizeable extent, to have their prescriptions filled, visit a doctor when ill, get recommended tests or follow up procedures because they had the largest out-of-pockets expenses for health care.
19. American patients had more negative care experiences than patients in any other country.
20. American patients more frequently reported going without care due to concerns about cost.

These errors have serious consequences, and one of the difficulties in the current U.S. health care system is that there are few built-in incentives for improving quality or safety. The Institute of Medicine's 2001 report estimates that "'medical errors' cause between cause between 44,000 and 98,000 deaths annually in hospitals in the United States of America—more than car accidents, breast cancer or AIDS" [World Health Organization]. Institutional mistakes are tracked for consequences, but no data are collected on noninstitutional (doctor's offices or clinics) errors, which could be equally high or even higher due to the lack of systematic monitoring.

Despite these twenty findings in which Americans received poorer or riskier care or didn't receive care at all, Americans did not rank the need for reforming the overall health system as highly as the Germans or the Canadians, two countries whose health systems outperform the American system by objective criteria. However, the majority of the sicker adults in all six countries thought that their health systems needed fundamental change or complete rebuilding. Nevertheless, American patients found more specific faults with and identified more errors made in their care than any of the patients in the other five nations.

The higher frequency of difficulties in health care delivery in the United States was confirmed by a World Health Organization [2000] study in which health experts ranked the health systems of 191 countries. The United States, in these experts' opinion, ranked 39th out of 191, the lowest ranking of any industrialized country. Although Blendon et al [2001] challenged the expert-opinion methodology by comparing the satisfaction rankings of the poor and the elderly in 17 industrialized nations with the experts' opinions and found substantial differences in the rankings. Nevertheless, the United States only ranked 14th out of 17 industrialized nations as ranked in satisfaction by the poor and elderly opinion surveys—not much of an improvement. Regardless of how a health care system is evaluated by the American public, the United States health system is not performing very well and its high costs and accessibility problems suggest that regardless of what Americans think fundamental system reform is needed.

TIME FOR REFORM OF THE AMERICAN HEALTH SYSTEM

Pressures for changing the fragmented system of health care financing in the United States are going to come from both the private and public sectors in the economy. We noted earlier the increased challenges that are being faced by employers, saddled with the highest health care costs in the world and obligations to their employees for the purchase of their health insurance while facing tougher worldwide competition from companies that do not have this obligation to their employees. American business is going to demand that the health insurance obligation be assumed by the public through some form of federal health insurance. As we shall see, another health care payer, the federal government, will also be faced with rising financial pressures that can be addressed only through fundamental reform of the American health care system and its method of financing care. Before we consider these rising pressures for change, however, a review of America's historical reluctance to adopt federal health insurance will be useful to gaining an understanding of why the 21ˢᵗ century could be different.

America's Historical Inability to Adopt Health Insurance
During the Progressive era early in the 20ᵗʰ century, the U.S. Congress first considered federal health insurance legislation by appointing in 1916 a committee to consider the concept of health insurance. However, it was not until the 1930s that the private market failed to generate a sufficient number of jobs and adequate retirement incomes for the aged and, thus, the public voted overwhelmingly for more liberal legislators to enact, with some bipartisan conservative support, a governmental program of unemployment and retirement insurance.

These social insurance programs could solve a problem that had become intolerable to a large majority of Americans. Nevertheless, President Franklin Delano Roosevelt, perhaps the greatest pragmatist of all American presidents, was unwilling to jeopardize the 1935 passage of social security legislation by including health insurance benefits. He was concerned that a large number of conservatives in the congressional Democratic majority, including the chairmen of both the Senate Finance and the House Ways and Means Committees, had different attitudes about health care. Because of the rapid pace of legislative activity, there had been no opportunity to marshal public support for health insurance. Without explicit expression of that support, Roosevelt must have believed that Congress and the public would place a deferential weight on the opinion of the medical community, and, indeed, the American Medical Association (AMA) was adamantly opposed to any governmental health insurance program [Skocpol].

Roosevelt's unwillingness to act without a popular mandate did not deter President Harry Truman's advocacy of federal health insurance in his 1948 presidential election campaign. Truman may have pulled off the biggest election upset in the 20th century by winning the presidency in 1948, but the AMA, in the one of the most successful public advertising campaigns ever waged by a special interest group, won the battle over health insurance. In hindsight an AMA executive concluded "the votes for compulsory national health insurance were never there," but the AMA's public relations firm "did a superb job and killed any possibility of legislation" [Campion].

However, in the 1960s when the AMA launched another public campaign against government health insurance for the aged, it could only postpone the inevitable. The majority of Americans wanted health insurance protection for the aged, but the electorate separated the issues of health insurance for the aged from universal coverage for all Americans. Seniors have a much greater need for care than younger Americans. Because of that greater utilization and the insurance practice of experience rating (charging premiums based on the insured's actual health costs), all but the very wealthy aged were being priced out of the private health insurance market in the late '50s and early '60s. Thus, a broad majority of Americans found the problem of health insurance for the aged to be intolerable. The private market could not solve the problem, and government action was taken.

Even with a popular mandate for the legislation, it should be noted that Wilbur J. Cohen, the assistant secretary for legislative affairs in and later Secretary of the Department of Health, Education, and Welfare, and Chairman Wilbur Mills of the House Ways and Means Committee, a fiscal conservative, who were asked by President Johnson in 1965 to draft the legislation, worked diligently to ensure bipartisan support. They carefully incorporated mandatory payroll taxes for financing the Medicare hospital benefits (Part A, the liberal's social insurance approach), voluntary premiums for the medical benefits (Part B based on a Republican proposal), and a federal-state program for Medicaid (the expansion of an idea proposed by the AMA) to ensure both liberal and conservative support and guarantee its passage.

The electorate favored a government health insurance program for the aged due to the active support of not only those 65 years of age and older, but also their children who were often responsible for financing their parents' health care expenses. The essential reason for failure to approve a governmental program for persons under age 65 is the lack of a large number of Americans who believed that their employer-sponsored health insurance needed to be replaced by a governmental program. Indeed, Medicare was designed to emulate that private health insurance program as closely as possible—to extend it, not to replace it. An imitation that Congress did so well that subsequent efforts to introduce market reform to the program were exceedingly difficult, as Newt Gingrich and his Republican cohorts learned in the 104th Congress in 1995.

In addition to their satisfaction with private insurance, much variability in public opinion stems from the fact that health care and health insurance needs are not randomly distributed across the population, as was noted earlier.

The concentration of health care need in a small segment of our population is an important reason for the failure to reach a political consensus on health insurance. The public may be sympathetic to government assistance for health care financing, but each proposal is judged in terms of individual needs and how it will affect the cost and benefits of the majority of Americans who already had health insurance through employer-sponsored plans. As noted, the fear of losing those benefits caused a spike in public support for the enactment of a governmental health insurance program in 1992.

The remaining two attempts to pass health insurance legislation prior to the Clintons' effort were played out without much fanfare for the general public. During 1970-74, the Congress was trying to enact legislation to contain the huge cost overruns from the Medicare-Medicaid programs. Consideration was given to federal health insurance as a means of instilling effective cost containment into the health care delivery system. In fact, during the post-Watergate leadership vacuum in 1974, President Gerald Ford almost worked out a compromise with Senator Edward Kennedy and Congressman Wilbur Mills for a mandated health insurance program that Steinmo and Watts [1995] described as having a "realistic chance to pass." However, Chairman Mills was unable to produce another miracle in the Ways and Means Committee, and the compromise died. If bipartisan legislative support could have been achieved in the Ways and Means Committee, there is little doubt that an active public campaign could have generated sufficient support for its passage. This may be the only time that liberals (primarily, organized labor) blocked passage of federal health insurance because they expected to do even better in the post-Watergate Congress in which a larger number of liberal members would be serving [Steinmo and Watts].

Similarly, the last pre-Clinton attempt came in the last year of the Carter Administration without bringing the issue to the public. It was only considered in the context of Democratic Party politics as part of Senator Kennedy's challenge to President Carter's party renomination in 1980. President Carter had already demonstrated his inability to work with a Democratically-controlled Congress. His hospital cost control measure was defeated in November 1979 by the House of Representatives with conservative Democrats voting with Republicans. No bipartisan support for health insurance could have been generated at that time, and it is also very doubtful that public support could have been mustered, in light of the success of Ronald Reagan's principal theme of running against government in the 1980 presidential campaign when distrust of government was running very high [Blendon et al 1994].

The most recent attempt to enact federal health insurance was done by President Clinton in 1993 and it proved to be a textbook case of what **not** to do to pass health insurance legislation. Because the issue had been effective in catching the public's attention and imagination in the '92 presidential election, the Clintons mistakenly emphasized an election-style campaign that gave a higher priority to the public instead of having serious discussions with members of the different political blocs represented in Congress. The appointment of First Lady Hillary Rodham Clinton to chair a presidential task force to formulate the Clinton Administration's health care reform proposal gave the issue a sense of the Administration's high priority for reform, but conducting the task force meetings in a confidential and exclusionary manner turned off many members of Congress whose support was needed for passage. What was needed for a legislative strategy was an open and inclusive process that could have begun the congressional campaign to win support for its passage. The congressmen and women of both parties who were knowledgeable and interested in health care should have been included in the formulation process both to seek their advice about what was needed and could be approved and to obtain their subsequent support.

Although the Democrats controlled the House and the Senate, Brady and Buckley [1995] argue that enactment of health care reform by the 103rd (1993-94) Congress required support of the median voters in both chambers. They identified nine conservative Democrats in the House and eight conservative Democrats plus four moderate Republicans in the Senate, who were needed to overcome a cloture vote. Once the issue of health insurance became a matter of partisan politics, there was little chance for passage because both liberal and conservative support was needed.

Despite the Clintons' frequent obeisance to the need for bipartisan efforts to pass health reform, their reform campaign from the start was extremely partisan. Republican members of Congress and their staffs, regardless of their interest or involvement in health reform, were systematically excluded from the presidential task force [Johnson and Broder, 131]. Their Democratic congressional supporters, with the Clintons' support, actively pursued the idea of attaching the reform proposal to the budget reconciliation process, which would only have required a simple majority in the Senate for passage. Although this tactic was blocked by Senator Robert Byrd's insistence that it was inappropriate to a topic of such legislative importance [Johnson and Broder, 126], its consideration was evidence that the Democrats were fully prepared to pursue health reform solely on a partisan basis. Senator Bob Dole, the Republican Majority Leader, had previously notified the president that no Republicans would vote for his budget proposal because of its proposed tax increases.

While the Democrats were fully prepared to make health reform a partisan issue, Republican House Minority Whip Newt Gingrich had been plotting since the spring of 1991 to use the defeat of a Democratic health reform proposal as the centerpiece of a Republican campaign to recapture control of the House of Representatives in 1994, if a Democrat were elected president in 1992 [Johnson and Broder, 39-40]. After Clinton's election Gingrich had ample time to solicit support from other conservative congressmen for his antigovernment campaign strategy. Until January or February 1994 there were still a sufficient number of uncommitted moderate Republicans, including Senator Dole, to have made the Gingrich proposal difficult to sell to the moderate wing of the party. The crucial tactical political resource in the health reform debate was, as Brady and Buckley suggested, moderate Senate Republicans, without whose support reform could not be enacted.

Partisanship can be extremely disruptive to the orderly consideration of legislation. The Clintons could have avoided making the issue partisan. If some moderate Republican support had been achieved early in the deliberative process, it would have been much more difficult for Gingrich to make the issue totally partisan in the summer of 1994. Nevertheless, there was still a reasonable chance for passage if the Clintons had clearly demonstrated that they were willing to make specific changes reflecting suggestions from big business, whose endorsement was essential to obtaining moderate Republican and conservative Democratic congressional support. Small business' concerted and politically effective opposition to mandated coverage had to be muted through a strategy to divide and conquer the business community. Mrs. Clinton and Ira Magaziner, the task force director, made numerous presentations to representatives of big business, but they failed to overcome or fully understand business' objections to the regulatory planks in President Clinton's reform plan [Johnson and Broder, 316-322].

When Congress reconvened in January 1994, two out of three national public opinion polls still showed that a majority of Americans favored the Clinton plan. Clinton utilized his January 25 State of the Union Message to a joint session of Congress as his third presentation of the plan to Congress. Instead of offering concessions to increase support for the proposal, the President chose to throw down the gauntlet by promising to veto any health insurance legislation that "does not guarantee every American private health insurance that can never be taken away" [Ifill]. Although there was a general statement of White House willingness to compromise on other aspects of the proposal, the President did not assure the interested parties that he had heard their concerns by responding directly through a series of modifications to the plan.

Clinton's unwillingness to compromise explicitly with business' concerns was the turning point in the debate. The week after the speech three business lobbying organizations—the Business Roundtable, the Chamber of Commerce, and the National Association of Manufacturers (NAM)—one by one withdrew their support for the mandated financing approach to health insurance. Thus, as soon as the President announced willingness to compromise on everything but the mandate, his legs were unexpectedly cut out from under his new position. Specific compromises were needed, not just a general willingness to compromise. The president of the NAM suggested "The business community got frustrated that the Clinton Administration was not responding to its substantive concerns about the scale and complexity of this bill" [Toner].

31

After early February the Clinton plan never again attained a majority favorable rating in any national public opinion poll. The Clinton plan, and with it the employer mandate, were dead, but the burial took several months and a great deal of work by five full committees and the majority leaders in both chambers. Congress would again be unable to pass health insurance legislation based on an employer-mandate, regardless of what the bill was called. Even worse, the issue of health care reform had become an overly partisan issue as soon as the Republicans believed that they could embarrass Clinton on failing to deliver on his strongest and most appealing campaign promise without suffering substantial public outrage themselves.

Requirements for Health Reform Legislation

Historical experience suggests that, even more than the case of other pieces of social legislation, the principal hurdle to the enactment of federal health insurance is bridging the ideological differences between conservative and liberal policy makers in the Congress. Bipartisan support is essential for the passage of health insurance, as Wilbur J. Cohen, President Johnson's legislative strategist, most particularly appreciated in shepherding Medicare with its universal entitlement for seniors through the Congress in 1965. A problem must be of such magnitude in the view of the public and the political parties that both liberals and conservatives are willing to settle for a bill with less than complete conformance to their ideological ideals. Both groups must either accept as their overriding goal the passage of health insurance or, at least, must believe that partisan opposition is contrary to their best interests. Once enacted, amendments to correct that bill's deficiencies could be passed as problems in the program become evident.

Before passage, liberals and conservatives must expect that the program's operating shortfalls will support their own remedial views. Management of public support for federal health insurance requires substantially less attention than the management of congressional support because there is a fundamental wellspring of support for health insurance that only requires nurturing until the political agreement has been reached. Then, the public campaign can be launched to bolster support for the compromise legislation—both Presidents Roosevelt and Clinton had it backwards. In past legislative struggles over health insurance, public opinion polls have been used as bullets in ideological sniping, but the public attitude has never been the crucial element in determining the outcome of those struggles. There has never been sufficient congressional and presidential agreement on putting markets and government together in a cohesive health insurance program to ask the public for its broad support of a unified proposal.

A Time for Confluence Between Conservatives and Liberals

The 2006 congressional elections, with the upcoming battle in the November congressional elections over control of Congress, will become so hard fought and partisan that the newly elected 110th (2007-08) Congress, regardless of which party is in control, is unlikely to be unable to pass a bipartisan health insurance proposal. However, the 2008 presidential election could well become the nation's first health insurance election, with both presidential candidates supporting their party's vision for health care reform in the United States. Democrats have since the 1930s supported their vision of a national social insurance model for health care as unfinished business of the New Deal, but what could persuade the more conservative Republicans to embrace a NHI proposal in their run for the presidency in 2008?

Ironically, the Republican interest in health insurance is likely to flow out of fiscal conservatism and a perceived need to eliminate the social insurance provision of Medicare as a means of regaining control over entitlements in the federal budget. The Republicans won't, however, call their plan national health insurance (NHI), but rather universal health insurance (UHI) to connote universal coverage of all Americans without identical benefits for every American and without having health care controlled by the government in Washington through a nationalistic formula. The Republican vision of UHI includes a market-controlled, not government-controlled, system of health care. Not only will the 2008 presidential election be about contrasting visions of health insurance, but more important, it will be about contrasting ideologies of government.

In such an ideological struggle the question turns on how bipartisan compromise is possible with such contrasting views. From a political standpoint, it is important to recognize that conservatives have the advantage on the issue, like Nixon's advantage in opening relations with China, because the passage of health insurance has been a goal for liberals since 1916. If the conservatives formulate a UHI proposal, there will always be a great temptation for some liberals to sign onto the legislation in order to accomplish what for many liberal congressmen or women has been a lifetime objective. The converse is not true with conservatives and it will be much more difficult to find conservative members of Congress that are willing to support liberal NHI legislation. Indeed, the tougher question to understand is why a large block of conservatives would agree to sponsor UHI legislation.

A Conservative Rationale for UHI

The short answer for the reasons conservative members of Congress are likely to introduce UHI legislative proposals is twofold: health care costs and national age demographics. Health care costs, after a brief period in the 1990s of slowing cost increases, have begun to increase at rates double the rate of inflation and "national health spending is forecast to continue growing faster than gross domestic product" [Heffler et al]. In addition, with the baby boom generation soon reaching seniority, the number of Medicare beneficiaries will expand substantially from about 12 percent of the population to 16.5 percent in 2020 and 20 percent in 2030. The effect of this aging of the American population can be seen in Table 1.4, which measures the percentage of payment for personal health care by different program sources. Government programs, Medicare and Medicaid, will grow from 20.5 percent of total personal health care payments in 1970 to nearly 45 percent of total payments in the projected cost of personal health care in 2014. The nation is moving inevitably from a predominately private health care financing system to a publicly financed health care system. It is the American demographics in the 21st century that are driving the increased cost of Medicare, and it is higher rate of increase in health care costs that is driving the increased cost of Medicaid.

TABLE 1.4
Source of Payment for Personal Health Care
For Selected Years in Percentages

Payer	1970	1980	1993	1997	2000	2004	2014*
Out-of-Pocket	39.6	27.2	18.8	16.9	16.9	15.1	14.0
Private Insurance	24.6	32.0	38.4	37.4	39.9	42.2	39.9
Medicare	12.2	17.3	19.2	21.9	19.8	19.8	24.4
Medicaid	8.3	12.1	15.8	16.5	17.7	18.8	20.2
Other**	15.3	11.4	7.8	7.3	5.7	4.1	1.5
Total	100.0	100.0	100.0	100.0	100.0	100.0	100.0

*Projected by the Office of the Actuary, Centers for Medicare and Medicaid Service, U.S Department of Health and Human Services.
**Miscellaneous private funds and payments by state and local government agencies.
Source: Data for 1970 to 2004 from C. Smith et al [2006] and projected data for 2014 from S Heffler et al [2005].

As we shall see, conservative legislators have some ideas about how cost controls might be used to contain the rate of increase in health care costs, but they can't change the population demographics—a higher percentage of Americans will continue to be older throughout the 21st century. Conservatives can, however, change the Medicare entitlement to reduce the future costs of the program by paying less in the future. The political dilemma is how to change the Medicare entitlement without enraging all the baby boom voters as well as the senior voters already enjoying Medicare benefits. The only possible political answer is to make the reform prospectively for future entitlement holders and keep the existing program for those currently 65 and over—politicians cannot renege on a promise made to such an active group of voters. The political problem is that the only prospective change in the Medicare program that will resolve its fiscal crisis is to change Medicare from a social insurance program (equal benefits for all persons regardless of their income) to an income related program, ensuring that government pays only for benefits beyond the financial capability of individual beneficiaries. Indeed, another way of looking at the future fiscal crisis is that the federal government will be going bankrupt paying for health benefits of persons who can afford to pay for all or at least a larger portion of their care. The nation, in the conservative viewpoint, can no longer afford the current middle class health entitlement.

Republicans are already picking at this approach for reducing net federal expenditures for Medicare by, as President Bush has done in his 2007 budget proposal, proposing to raise the Part B medical benefit premiums for higher income American seniors. However, the net savings in Medicare expenditures by the income-related premium approach are minor in comparison to redefining all Medicare benefits in relationship to the beneficiary's income. Lower income American seniors would retain the current level of benefits, but middle and upper income seniors, in the future, would receive proportionally less benefits, or conversely, would be expected to pay for services out of their own resources to the extent that they are financially able.

An income-related set of health insurance benefits is totally consistent with the conservative approach to health care cost containment. Conservatives believe that marketplace controls are the most effective means of restraining health care costs. It is for this reason that Republicans have supported Health Saving Account (HSA) provisions in the tax code to encourage Americans to purchase health care services in the same prudent way they purchase other goods and services in contrast to first-dollar health insurance, which puts the purchasing burden on the insurer rather than the consumer. In a perfect analogy to the minimal nature of the savings in the income-related premium, HSAs have only been minimally effective in cost saving, with only a few million Americans buying them in 2006 (see pages 21-22).

The final reason for conservatives to support universal health insurance has already been mentioned. A key constituency of the Republican Party is business, which is discovering that employee health benefits are a great disadvantage in global competition in which foreign competitors do not directly bear these health care costs and are from countries with lower health care costs than in the United States. Passing UHI will get employers off the hook for these costs. In addition, employees, themselves, are less enamored with employee health benefits as more employers require their workers to pick up an ever larger share of the health insurance premiums, or even the whole premium. Employees can no longer be expected to be used as opponents of governmentally provided health insurance as the Republicans did, through a clever advertising campaign by commercial insurers, to defeat the Clinton health reform proposal in 1994.

One shortcoming for conservatives of the income-related entitlement is limiting its application. Why shouldn't all Americans, regardless of age, be entitled to government health insurance that pays for financially unaffordable health care, is the question that under 65 voters will be asking in discussions of changing the Medicare entitlement to an income-related benefit. There is no good answer to this question short of enacting a universal income-related health insurance program for all Americans, which is why reforming the Medicare program will become an argument for enacting UHI.

But making more limited benefits universally available only extends federal financial problems unless general taxes are raised to cover these additional costs. However, a substantial part of the necessary tax increase can be achieved by taxing employer-paid health insurance benefits. Many employees will no longer want employer-sponsored health insurance because the new universal government health insurance benefit can replace that benefit. These employees will, however, demand that the employers' savings be paid to them in the form of increased (and taxable) wages. Employers, who will be relieved of an expense that is projected to increase substantially in cost in future years, will be hard pressed to refuse these demands. Other workers may want to continue their employer-provided health insurance for the costs that will be their responsibility under the government plan. These workers will have to pay taxes on the cost of such a benefit and they cannot expect their employers to raise their wages, as they did for the others who gave up the benefit. An alternative scenario is for employers to raise all employee wages by the cost of the health insurance benefits and then charge those employees who want to continue a lower cost (by at least the amount of the federal government's larger share of health care costs) health insurance coverage.

In all likelihood there will be enough congressional conservatives that will see sufficient advantages to proposing UHI to more than offset the disadvantage of needing to increase income taxes to partially finance a new UHI program. Income-related universal health insurance will give conservatives a program: for letting the market work its competitive wonders at reducing the rate of health cost increases, for creating greater equity among all Americans in access to health services and health insurance, for bailing out a very important constituency—business, and for restoring the Republican party's record as being fiscally responsible.

MAJOR REFORM VERSUS TINKERING

Because we have already established that the American health care system is badly broken and seen that there are political reasons for both conservatives and liberals to introduce legislative proposals for national or universal health insurance, it may seem redundant to step back and discuss whether major reform like NHI or UHI is really needed to fix the broken system. However, many, especially conservatives, will continue to argue that incremental reforms, tinkering, will be sufficient to repair these system defects and that national health insurance legislation, in any form, represents an unwise and unnecessary step toward big government. The latest tinkering proposal is President Bush's proposal for enhanced tax incentives for Health Savings Accounts (HSAs) that was announced in his January 30, 2006 State of the Union address. HSAs may be used to illustrate the limited effects tinkering reforms will have on the health care system.

What Are HSAs?

HSAs have been available since 2003. When Congress passed the Medicare drug benefit, it also approved a tax benefit for employees who purchase high deductible health insurance and establish health savings accounts from which medical payments for the deductible may be paid. The idea was to provide a tax benefit to encourage the purchase of high deductible health insurance rather than the more traditional first-dollar health insurance coverage. It was argued that consumers will be better purchasers of care if they are responsible for a greater share of their health care costs—consumers would be more price-sensitive in selecting providers and approving medical procedures. Only about 1 million Americans initially took advantage of this program, but that total has increased to about 3 million HSAs by January 2006, which is a small fraction of the nearly 180 million people covered by private health insurance. Freudheim [2006] speculated that many purchasers of the high deductible insurance did so simply because "the plan looked cheap or they had no other insurance option, for about half the purchasers did not establish the savings accounts to take advantage of the tax-free earnings.

President Bush's new plan would substantially increase the tax benefits of savings accounts, providing tax-free earnings as long as the proceeds of the account is spent on health care needs, which is broader than the 2003 law that limited tax-free expenditure to paying expenses incurred in meeting the deductible, a tax credit to offset payroll taxes for those buying the high-deductible insurance themselves in the non-group market, and bigger limits on the accounts—$2,700 for an individual or $5,400 for a family each year. Indeed, the annual limit is so large that many banks and investment companies are promoting the accounts as investment vehicles without any concerns about health care expenditures [Dash]. The only requirement to qualify for the tax benefits is the purchase of a health insurance policy with a high deductible: in 2006, at least $1050 for an individual or $2,100 for a family. The money in the health savings accounts can be used to pay for health care expenditures making up the deductible or health insurance premiums, or higher income individuals may pay those expenses out of other funds to gain the maximum tax savings, but eventually the funds will have to be disbursed on health care costs to obtain the maximum tax benefit.

The theory behind the tax incentive is to get more Americans to buy higher deductible health insurance plans (it discourages first-dollar coverage) so that they will become more price conscious purchasers of health care to put more pressure on health care providers to minimize the cost of providing health services. The theory may prove to be valid for those individuals interested in tax-free investment, but are there likely enough of these individuals in our economy to be of great significance in the overall health care market? Lower income Americans are unlikely to the have excess cash to invest in the health savings accounts and, of course with our progressive income tax system, receive smaller tax benefits from the tax exclusion. Employers support the program as a means of reducing the cost of their employee health insurance because high deductible insurance is generally cheaper than more comprehensive health insurance [Francis and Schultz], but their support won't increase HSA coverage unless part of the employer insurance savings are paid as tax-free savings to the employees' health savings accounts to encourage investment in HSAs.

What Are the Likely Reform Benefits of HSAs?

Even if all persons under 65 that are insured through private health insurance policies switched to the high deductible plans and, according to their individual financial capabilities, invested in HSAs, the maximum effect of the program would be to bring a greater level of price competition to health care providers, which could contribute to reducing the rate of health care cost increases in the United States. The HSA plan would do nothing in solving the nation's access problems— uninsured individuals would still be uninsured—and the nation's health delivery system would still be one of the riskiest health systems among industrialized nations. The HSA proposal is single-faceted, only focusing on the cost problem.

Indeed, it could have substantial impact on health care costs if all eligible private health insurance purchasers bought high deductible coverage, but its proponents more realistically expect much less market penetration. President Bush more modestly hopes that his enhanced tax incentives will encourage 21 million HSAs by 2010, which suggests that nearly 160 million others will continue to purchase first-dollar or more comprehensive health insurance coverage. With such a limited number of HSA subscribers, even the hoped for health care cost savings are likely to be greatly dissipated.

The HSA proposal is as good as any other tinkering-scale reform plan, but it cannot provide a vehicle for broad reform of the U.S. health care delivery and financing system or even its more limited goal of restructuring the health insurance market. Too much is wrong with the American health care system to expect any tinkering proposal to overcome all that is broken. The problems are systemic and the only way to reform the American system is to start all over and rebuild both the health care delivery and financing systems.

The fundamental structural defects in the health care health insurance markets would have required careful redesign to overcome. Instead the American political system in a reckless and unplanned manner, stumbled into providing a tax incentive that encouraged first dollar health insurance coverage and built private health insurance into private sector dominance of financing health care in the United States. Even when it added public financing mechanisms, government patterned them closely on private models. There is a profound difference between a private sector economy in an industry and a market-driven sector. Although the nation cannot have a market-driven industry without a strong private sector, the health industry is only private-sector-dominated and what is needed is a market-driven industry. In the next chapter, a full consideration of the problems in the existing health care and insurance markets will be made.

REDESIGNING AMERICA'S HEALTH CARE SYSTEM

The remainder of the book will consider the process of redesigning America's health care system. In the next chapter, Chapter 2, the prototypes, a free-market or a government-operated health care system, will be described and compared, after a full-scale analysis of the health care and health insurance markets has been conducted. Chapter 3 will consider the economic differences between the two reform systems. Chapter 4 will consider how the politics of choosing between two systems is likely to and should play out. And finally, Chapter 5 will consider two possible futures for the American health care system—the status quo without any further government intervention or a market-driven health care system—and why the single-payer, government system of reform drops out. The overall objective of the book is to create awareness of the problems in the American health care system and compare the possible ways in which the American health care system can be rebuilt into a more effective, efficacious, equitable, and cost efficient system.

BIBLIOGRAPHY

Anderson, G.F., Reinhardt, U.E., Hussy, P.S., and Petrosyan, V., "It's the Prices, Stupid: Why the United States Is So Different From Other Countries," *Health Affairs*, Vol. 22, No. 3 (May/ June, 2003), pp. 89-105.

Berk, M.L., and Monheit, A.C.,"The Concentration of Health Expenditures, Revisited," *Health Affairs*, Vol. 20, No. 2 (March/April 2001), pp. 9-18.

Blendon, R.J., Kim, M., and Benson, J.M., "The Public Versus the World Health Organization on Health Service Performance," *Health Affairs*, Vol. 20, No. 3 (May/June) 2001), pp. 10-20.

Blendon, R.J., Marttila, J., Benson, J.M., Shelter, M.C., Connolly, F.J., and Kiley, T. "The Beliefs and Values Shaping Today's Health Care Reform Debate," *Health Affairs,* Vol. 13, No. 1 (Spring 1994) 274-284.

Brady, D.W., and Buckley, K.M., "Health Care Reform in 103rd Congress: A Predictable Failure," *Journal of Health Politics, Policy and* Law, Vol. 20 (Summer 1995), pp. 447-454.

Burnstein, H.R., Lipsitz, S.R., and Brennan, T.A., "Socioeconomic Status and Risk for Substandard Care," *Journal of the American Medical* Association, Vol 68 (Nov. 4, 1992), pp. 2383-2387.

Campion, F.D., *The AMA and U.S Health Policy, Since 1940*, Chicago: Chicago Review Press, 1984.

Dash, E., "Savings Accounts for Health Costs Attract Wall St.," *New York Times*, January 27, 2006.

"Drake, D.F., *Reforming the Health Care Market: An Interpretive Economic History*, Washington, DC: Georgetown University Press, 1994.

Francis, T., and Schultz, E.E., "Health Accounts Have Benefits for Employers," *Wall Street Journal*, February 3, 2006.

Freudheim, M., "Prognosis is Mixed for Health Savings, *New York Times*, January 26, 2006.

Heffler, S., Smith, S. Keeham, S., Borger, C., Clemens, M.K., and Truffer, C., "Trends: U.S. Health Care Spending Projections for 2004-2014," *Health Affairs – Web Exclusive*, W5 (February 23, 2005), 74-85.

Ifill, G., "Clinton Offers a Domestic Renewal Plan." *New York Times*, January 26, 1994.

Johnson, H., and Broder, D.S., *The System, The American Way of Politics at the Breaking Point*, Boston: Little, Brown and Company, 1996.

Lillie-Blanton, M., and Hoffman, C., "The Role of Health Insurance Coverage in Reducing Racial/Ethnic Disparities in Health Care," *Health Affairs*, Vol. 24, No.2 (March/April 2005), pp. 398-408.

Organization for Economic Cooperation and Development (OECD), http://oecd.org./home/ 0,2987,en_2649_201185_1_1_1_1_1,00.html.

Roos, N.P., Shapiro, E., and Tate, R., "Does a Small Minority of Elderly Account for a Majority of Health Expenditures?" *Milbank Quarterly*, Vol. 67 (1989), pp. 347-369.

Schoen, C., Osborn, R., Trang Hunynh, P., Doty, M., Zapert, K., Peugh, J. and Davis, K., "Taking the Pulse of Health Care Systems: Experiences of Patients with Health Problems in Six Countries," *Health Affairs—Web Exclusive*, W5 (November 3, 2005) 509-525.

Skocpol, T., "Is the Time Finally Ripe? Health Insurance in the 1990s," *Journal of Health Politics, Policy and Law*, Vol. 18 (Fall 1993), pp. 531-550.

Smith, C., Cowan, C., Heffler, S., Catlin, A., and the National Health Accounts Team, "Trends: National Health Spending in 2004: Recent Slowdown Led by Prescription Drug Spending," *Health Affairs*, Vol. 25, No. 1 (January/February 2006), pp. 186-196.

Steinmo, S., and Watts, J., "It's the Institutions, Stupid! Why Comprehensive National Health Insurance Always Fails in America," *Journal of Health Politics, Policy and Law*, Vol. 20 (Summer 1995), pp. 329-372.

Toner, R., "Shift in Health Strategy: Given Details to Congress," *New York Times*, February 13, 1994.

U.S. Department of Health and Human Services, *Health, United States, 2005*, Washington, DC: Superintendent of Documents, 2005.

World Health Organization, "Quality of care: patient safety, Report by the Secretariat," March 23, 2002.

"The World Health Report 2000," Press release, June 21, 2000, http://www.who.int/whr/2000/en/press_release.htm.

CHAPTER 2
Reform Prototypes:
A Market-Driven or a
Single-Payer Health System

If the American health system is broken and, thus, federal health insurance—either NHI or UHI—is required to fix it, there are a whole host of different proposals that could be made. And a discussion of any insurance program can be exceedingly complex. However, in our exposition, only two fundamental approaches, a market-driven system (UHI) and a single-payer (NHI) system, will be discussed. Even in discussing these two prototypes, there are almost an infinite number of variations and permutations that can be employed in constructing the national or universal health insurance proposals. For example, there can be variety of different health insurance benefit packages (what's covered by the insurance). To simplify our discussion the current Medicare benefit package, including drug benefits, will be assumed for both approaches. However, where the positions of the two are known to differ from the simplifying assumptions, those differences will be pointed out.

The two approaches that have been selected represent the extremes into which most other possibilities can be placed. Both are or have been proposed as health insurance systems. Both require greater but different kinds of governmental intervention into the American health system. Finally and crucially, each takes very contrary views of the role of markets in health care delivery and financing. Advocates of the single-payer system recommend that the private health care market be totally abandoned in the operation of its preferred governmental health delivery system, while the market-driven approach is based on the presumption that private markets perform a vital function in the allocation of resources, but the current health care market has structural defects that can be corrected by government intervention through a system of income-related health insurance.

Because of the centrality of these two opposing views about the health care market, this chapter begins with a discussion of the reasons for the market imperfections in the way the health care market has been structured. The significant questions for the reader that are raised in this discussion are: Can the structural defects in the health care market be fixed and is fixing the market a worthwhile social objective? After attempting to resolve those questions, the chapter proceeds to describe the two prototype reform systems, without economic or political comment. Those considerations follow in order in the next two chapters.

THE IMPERECT HEALTH CARE MARKET

Economists have long recognized that doctors know much more about health care than consumers can possibly understand. That difference in knowledge between buyer and seller is just one of the ways in which the health care market differs from other classic markets. However, in this section it is argued that the inefficiencies in the health market can be explained by focusing on market structure as the critical flaw in the pre-1985 market, allowing producers to dominate the market in ways that extended beyond the knowledge differential between consumers and producers. A producer-dominated market is defined as one in which the market is structured to give producers greater influence over the demand for their product as well as the conditions for producing the product than in a competitively organized or even monopolized market. In a producer-dominated market, both higher prices are charged and more services are provided than in a price-competitive market with cost sensitive consumers facing a limited budget. Monopolists produce fewer goods than would be produced in a competitive market to be able to charge higher prices for those fewer goods, and thus earn higher profits. However, in a producer-dominated market both more units are sold and a higher price per unit is paid than in a price-competitive market. That is, the theory predicts that, when price competition replaces producer dominance in the health care market, lower unit prices will be charged for specific medical services and fewer units of those services will be sold. However, the out-of-pocket share of the lower cost medical services paid by consumers may rise as health insurance coverage is restructured.

The domination thesis suggests that when the consumer knowledge deficiency is coupled with a market structure that makes the consumer insensitive to product costs so that consumption decisions are not influenced by **differences** in producer costs, then this producer advantage is greater than simply the effects of producers possessing greater knowledge. Further, the dominance structure makes it very difficult for the market, itself, to develop alternatives for educating consumers about medical decision-making; there is no incentive for consumers to educate themselves.

Producer domination of a market is a utopia for the producer, and unless the market is restructured to introduce price competition, the domination normally cannot be eliminated. The underlying market dynamic in a free-market economy is to attempt to disrupt producer domination through counter efforts in the rest of the economy, either new entrants or new buying techniques, but these changes would be of no avail without price competition. Nirvana for doctors and hospitals has lasted a very long time because of the difficulty payers (employers) had in finding a method of introducing price competition.

That the U.S. health care market was producer-dominated was not apparent until after selective contracting implicit to managed-care organizations caught on as a purchasing technique for employer-sponsored private health insurers in the 1980s and, more strongly in the '90s, and the first primitive forms of price competition were established among health care providers. The new behaviors that were emerging in the more competitive health market in the '90s could have brought a sea change in market control of the health care industry had consumers not objected to some of the limitations imposed by managed care mechanisms; managed care did not provide any rewards, only penalties, to consumers.

The next section describes the historical circumstances that permitted hospitals and doctors to dominate the U.S. health market and explains the role health insurance design and marketing had in increasing the demand for health services, presents evidence of the provider domination of the market, and then describes how employers finally solved the health market puzzle and tried to end provider dominance by finding a method of purchasing health services that forced providers to compete on the basis of price. Doctors and hospitals, however, soon persuaded consumers to abandon the elements of managed care that had almost ended producer dominance of the health care industry.

The Happenstance of Provider Domination

With strong support from the federal government and the acquiescence of employers, doctors and hospitals held price competition in the health care industry at bay through two separate but related agreements that were reached, first, by doctors and hospitals around the time of World War I, and then, between health care providers and health insurers during the Great Depression. These two agreements proved to be a most enduring anticompetitive compact with violation of antitrust law for only a brief time and probably **without** any understanding of how these agreements disrupted market competition. It did, however, require a great deal of political moxie and bluster that the American Medical Association was able to create.

Most economists will no doubt remain skeptical that physicians acted in any way other than an income maximizing manner. Although doctors may have intuitively recognized the income advantage of maintaining free choice, the AMA policies about health insurance stressed the importance of maintaining trust in the physician-patient relationship, and expressed grave concerns about the possibility of insurance disrupting that relationship [Dickinson 1946]. Even skeptics will have to agree that the behavior of some managed care organizations may have exceeded the physicians' worst 1930s fears.

The first agreement was an accord between hospitals and physicians. It was accepted throughout the country voluntarily and gave physicians broad control over the medical affairs of the hospital, including a separate organization that controlled the appointment of individual staff members, their practice privileges within the institution, and the authority to discipline members, as well as the right of all staff members to use hospital facilities without charge. Hospitals became "the physician's workshop" for those physicians who were selected for medical staff membership. What was not recognized as a formal part of this accord until the 1970s, when it gradually was discontinued, was that the physicians without staff privileges would not compete with services offered by the hospital. Thus, physicians who were able to obtain staff appointments competed with each other in the hospital, but the physicians without staff privileges did not compete for those hospital services until the 1970s.

The second agreement, the insurance accord, was reached in the 1930s when economic conditions led community hospitals, as a marketing ploy, to start prepayment plans in which a specified number of days of hospital care were offered for a small monthly payment. Hospital prepayment quickly spread around areas of the country, and surgeons, who then accounted for 75 percent of all hospital admissions, also began to organize similar plans for physician services.

Organized medicine aggressively opposed the establishment of voluntary health insurance, largely because general practitioners (GPs) objected to voluntary health insurance as a threat to their already perilous economic circumstances from competition with physicians trained in scientific medicine. Leaders of the medical community worked out a compromise that imposed two conditions on provider-organized health insurance programs. First, the plans had to be cooperative, not competitive, so that all physicians practicing in the market would be eligible for payment of health insurance benefits. Or stated as the principle was marketed, consumers must have the right to "free choice of physician" for the health insurance plan to be acceptable to organized medicine. The second condition was a compromise between GPs and surgeons, who favored voluntary insurance and organized the Blue Shield (doctor) plans during this period. The compromise limited insured physician benefits to those services associated with the hospital, which excluded health insurance benefits for physician services performed out of the hospital. That exclusion proved costly to generalists, and it distorted the distribution of specialists practicing medicine in the United States [Drake 1994, 67-71].

When shortages of GPs and family physicians developed in the '60s and '70s, larger federal grant programs, largely to medical schools, were approved to support the growth in physician supply. These programs had been constructed to encourage the education of more primary-care physicians, even though the newly educated physicians chose specialization in ever larger numbers [Freymann 1974, 355-358]. When physician specialists needed more support personnel, Congresses and presidents passed health manpower training funds for the education of nurses and medical technicians. The federal government supported the distorted system without understanding how it was contributing to an out-of-balance health care market.

Federal Ratification and Extension

Although the federal government in 1944, through antitrust litigation, struck down the prohibition against physician participation in competitively-organized health plans, most other government activities, during and after World War II, greatly strengthened these anticompetitive agreements, which served as the basis for organizing and promoting the employer-sponsored health insurance system as the dominant health care financing system for Americans. The local medical societies' tactics in discouraging involvement in competitive health insurance plans ranged from moral suasion through policy pronouncements attacking "contract medicine," direct economic competition through the operations of Blue Shield medical insurance plans, to expulsion of the contract physicians from the local medical society. This tactic was especially devastating to the competitive plans when local hospitals required medical society membership as a condition for hospital staff memberships and privileges. The practice was subsequently found to violate provisions of the Sherman Antitrust Act in the landmark case of American Medical Association v. United States 317 U.S. 519 (1943) involving the Group Health Association of Washington. During the 1940s and '50s a number of antitrust suits redressed grievances stemming from illegal harassment by medical societies of group practices and competitive plans; e.g., the Group Health Cooperative of Puget Sound in 1951 resorted to litigation to stop the King County Medical Society from boycotting its members.

The primary unintentional and unplanned government support for the hospitals and doctors became the basis on which the employer-sponsored health insurance system was organized and promoted as the dominant health care financing system for employed and wealthier Americans. During World War II wage and price controls, employers were granted an exception from wage controls for labor's contractual fringe benefits and later a tax exemption to labor fringe benefits. These exemptions proved to be a boost for union membership by the inclusion of fringes as a central element in the collective bargaining arena and as a result for private health insurance, which had just begun to be marketed in the late 1930s. This development, plus the inherent appeal of health insurance, led to more than a ten-fold increase in the number of persons enrolled in hospital insurance programs by 1965. Enrollments rose from less than 10 million in 1940 to nearly 130 million, or about 72 percent of the population in 1965. Almost two-thirds of that number had additional insurance coverage for surgical benefits and nearly one-half had regular medical coverage.

The prototype employer-sponsored plan in the '40s and '50s had included low-dollar deductibles and comprehensive, hospital-related service benefits, with the freedom to choose any provider. The Blues were basically cooperatives organized by producers to market and finance their services. The Blues based their premiums on the average cost of care in particular markets, the so-called "community rating" method. However, commercial insurance carriers, who did not whole-heartedly enter into the market until sale through employment had reduced the risk of adverse selection, found that they could accept organized medicine's two constraints and successfully compete with Blue Cross/Shield by identifying firms that were likely to have lower than average health costs. They offered premium pricing based on the actual experience of those firms' lower health care costs. This method of pricing, called "experience rating," gradually led to the loss of the Blues' healthiest clients and forced them to abandon community rating to compete with the commercial carriers. The switch to experience rating in the private market caused an unanticipated political problem for the insurers because experience rating led to very high premiums for retired persons.

These plans with their enfranchisement of health services, with little out-of-pocket expense, came to be employees' most cherished benefit. Consequently, in the late '50s and early '60s when the largest number of American workers left employment since the Great Depression, those retirees faced the higher premiums based on experience rating, which few could afford. A political crisis in financing care for the aged erupted. Medicare was fashioned to resemble as closely as possible their employer-sponsored health insurance plans, administered through the same insurance carriers with the promise not to interfere in the practice of medicine.

These programs had been constructed to emulate politically popular private health insurance plans without recognizing that private health insurance had, "For all practical purposes...no controls on the providers. Hospitals were paid cost or charges, whichever was lower; physicians were paid their usual and customary fees" [Anderson, 263], reflecting the producer-cooperative origins of private health insurance. All of the conditions that organized medicine had sought in the pre-World War II development of hospital and health insurance had become integral parts of the federal health entitlement.

The direction and emphasis for the U.S. health care system had been established, and, because of the political popularity of these programs, subsequent federal actions continued to support hospital-centered, specialized, and high-tech health care. When the Medicare-Medicaid programs were implemented, the U.S. health insurance market for hospital and doctor services reached the saturation point of low-dollar coverage. The Rand Health Insurance Experiment, a large study of 5,809 people randomly selected, demonstrated that health care consumers are quite sensitive to out-of-pocket costs with the finding that health care costs were nearly one-third less for persons with relatively large deductibles, or at least 25 percent coinsurance provisions, than for individuals having free care (first-dollar coverage) [Newhouse et al, 1993].

Even the modest Medicare deductibles and copayments encouraged some increased utilization of health services. However, more than 70 percent of the Medicare beneficiaries in 1991 also had private medigap coverage; 36.1 percent directly purchased, 35.3 percent were Medicaid recipients, and 3.7 percent were enrolled in a Medicare HMO program [Levit et al 1992 and McMillan]. Further, the Medicare cost sharing liability to its beneficiaries, which for more than 70 percent can be billed to other public or private insurers, to its beneficiaries has also been dropping from 18.0 percent of all Medicare expenditures in 1977 to 15.2 percent in 1992 [HHS], as more physicians accepted assignment as a basis of payment. With such coverage, the percentage of Medicare beneficiaries who utilize health services each year rose from less than half in 1974 [Lazenby and Letsch] to 81.6 percent in 1994 [Levit et al 1996a].

Relationships for Provider Dominance
The two key market relationships that established provider dominance were low-dollar deductibles and pretax financing of health insurance (influencing demand) and free choice of providers without any market effect of price differences. The key political event to achieving market domination occurred with the passage of Medicare in 1965 for senior citizens based on the1930s health insurance model

that maintained and expanded the two key market relationships to a very price sensitive and higher health care utilizing age group. Although the 65 and over represented only 9.5 percent of the population in 1965, 23.8 percent of all health care spending was devoted to this consumer group [Fisher 1980]. By 1987, this group represented 12.2 percent of the population and consumed 36.3 percent of the nation's health care [Waldo et al].

Although provider influence in altering the demand for health care had been much less direct and more fortuitous than their influence on supply controls, the effect on increasing the demand for health care services was, nevertheless, significant and targeted specifically at increasing the demand for physician and hospital services. Making the sale of health insurance to employers, rather than directly to employees, proved to be a classic marketing device of shielding direct costs of insurance from the normal buyer tension of having to consider the purchases in terms of the limit imposed on the quantities of other goods and services that could be bought. Further, it protected insurers from adverse selection (persons with the higher level of health care illnesses purchasing health insurance and healthier individuals do not) by having all employees enroll, the preponderant healthy as well as the higher-risk group that really needed insurance. To have the federal government provide tax subsidies by permitting the purchase to be made with pretax dollars was simply an extra bonus for hospitals and physicians. Low user fees, and the concentration of benefits on doctor and hospital services, were natural products of the provider-cooperative origins of health insurance.

A long-term concerted campaign by organized provider groups was waged on the supply side of the market for the maintenance of the free choice of provider. This provision was the most critical to provider dominance of the health care market because it protected doctors and hospitals from price competition within their ranks. As long as most consumers with health insurance could freely choose to receive care from any doctor or hospital in the marketplace with the combination of minor differences in out-of-pocket fees, it was virtually impossible to create any pressure on providers to compete on the basis of price for their services. The free choice of hospitals and physicians, combined with small user fees, eliminated price competition in this segment of the health market. It is the multiplicative effect of free choice of provider in conjunction with the high insurance coverage that led to provider dominance. Newhouse [1978], focusing on the insurance contract, noted the lack of price competition, and his later study of market erosion [1988] detected a change in behavior in the 1980s.

The overall effect of the design and marketing of private insurance was the creation of a health care financing system that anesthetized cost sensitivities of the American health care consumer by minimizing the direct consumer payments for health insurance coverage and service user fees. When Congress bought the whole package as the health entitlement for the poor and the aged, and later added the disabled and those persons with renal failure, true producer dominance of the industry was achieved. Because the AMA opposed Medicare throughout its nine-year congressional debate, further doubt is cast on producer dominance being established by deliberate conspiratorial action by the medical profession. A "blind luck" explanation is more consistent with the facts.

However, over this 50 year period the health care market had become an environment for comfortable, collegial, noncompetitive relationships among health care providers. The physician was the unchallenged captain of the team of care providers and the doctors' workshop was the community hospital which had become the center for the practice of scientific medicine. Biomedical research, medical education, and health care facilities were all generously supported by grants from the federal government. Physicians had earned trust in their profession as whole and individually with their patients. As a result, the political popularity of American medicine and the adroitness of its demands provided ample federal support for doctors and hospitals to achieve market dominance.

Without understanding the consequences, consumers (voters) embraced "free" employer-sponsored or government entitlement for low-dollar comprehensive health insurance, which has financed all of the post-1940 expansion in health care spending. That spending rose from less than 4 percent of GDP in the '30s to 11.2 percent in 1988, the peak year of market penetration at 87.1 percent, as measured by the percentage of Americans covered by health insurance. Doctors and hospitals avoided price competition in the health care market until employers started to challenge employees' right to a costless choice of provider.

Primary Evidence of Dominance

The argument of the dominance hypothesis is that the lack of price competition in health care was a major cause for the extraordinary rate of increase in health care spending in this period and a primary reason for the United States spending so much more on health care than other developed nations. In a producer-dominated market, market outcomes measure producer, not consumer, choice, and the higher proportion of spending on health care in the United States than in other developed countries is indicative of producer dominance, which raised costs more than the asymmetric possession of knowledge by consumers and physicians in the medical markets of these other developed nations.

When consumers are not sensitive to cost differentials in choosing doctors or hospitals, then providers do not have the competitive market incentive to minimize costs. Without market pressure to keep costs below their rivals', providers can give greater weight to noneconomic considerations, such as professional and personal standards in designing their care programs. It also meant that physician effort in maintaining high quality and patient safety standards was limited to activities low in physician involvement. Such behavior is generally consistent with Feldman and Sloan's [1988] suggestion that "variations in demand induced by physicians' discretionary behavior may be due to systematic increases in quality or amenities." The only qualification is that physicians are unlikely to encourage programs for quality enhancement that involve substantial impediments to their preferred practice style. It is also consistent with Robinson and Luft's [1987] conclusion that hospitals competed by increasing services and facilities to attract better medical staffs. Further, it permitted U.S. physicians to earn higher incomes and see fewer patients than physicians in other developed countries [Drake 1994, 138].

Although the provider-supported market structure was firmly entrenched in the health insurance marketplace by the conclusion of World War II, the implications of cost subsidizations and the shielding of direct cost effects on family budgets occurred gradually over the postwar period as private health insurance coverage grew. After the passage of Medicare in 1965, the full effects of producer dominance can be observed.

By dividing the industry into two sectors—the hospital-physician sector including other professional services, and the rest of the health care industry—the effects of provider dominance should be apparent because the other sector did not directly benefit from these tactics to structure the market. Consequently, the dominance theory suggests that the hospital-physician sector should have been able to achieve much larger revenue increases than the other health sector, especially after 1965.

Table 2.1 confirms the gradual buildup of dominance by reporting the hospital-doctor partnership's market share of the health care industry's revenues, the percentage of consumer out-of-pocket (direct) costs for hospital-physician services and the percentage for other health services, and the price-level adjusted rate of annualized growth for the hospital-physician and other health service revenues for, generally, in five-year periods from 1960 to 2004. The market share of health industry revenues earned by the hospital-doctor sector rose from 64.3 in 1965 to 71.3 percent in 1985, a 10.9 percent increase in market share, as third-party revenue payments increased from 63.2 percent (the inverse of direct patient payments) in 1960 to 85.7 percent in 1985. While the rest of the health industry was losing market share, it was, nevertheless, picking up third-party revenues, which rose from 12.2 to 45.9 percent of their total revenues between 1960 and 1985 and since 1985 through 2003 increased faster than in the hospital-doctor sector. But only in the period 1985 to 2000 in which managed care reached prominence did the non-hospital and physician sector gain 9.1 percent in market share.

TABLE 2.1
Comparison of Hospital and Doctor Sector
With the Rest of the Health Industry
For Selected Years, 1960-2004

	Spending on Hospital and Doctors			Other Health Spending	
Year	% of Industry	% Out-of-Pocket	Real Rate of Annual Growth	% Out-of-Pocket	Real Rate of Annual Growth
1960	64.4	36.8	6.9%	87.8	3.9%
1965	64.3	35.5	6.8	81.3	6.4
1970	67.3	21.4	8.0	75.2	7.1
1975	69.1	19.1	5.7	65.4	4.0
1980	71.1	15.0	6.0	58.3	2.9
1985	71.3	14.3	5.7	54.1	5.5
1990	71.2	13.7	6.3	48.4	6.5
1995	68.8	11.3	2.6	41.1	5.7
2000	65.2	7.9	5.8	34.8	7.7
2004	65.6	7.1	8.3	30.4	6.3

SOURCE: Levit et al [2002, 1996b, 1992, and 1985] and C. Smith for the 2004 data. All growth rates have been adjusted for inflation and are annualized. The hospital and doctor sector also includes other professional services to recognize physician ownership of many independent laboratories and other freestanding ambulatory facilities.

During the first 25-year period, the hospital-physician segment grew, in real terms, 4.686 times, which was 33.7 percent more than the rest of the industry's real growth of 3.51, or a 6.4 percent average rate of real growth for the hospital-physician sector versus a 5.2 percent growth rate for the rest of the industry. After 1985 when market conditions in the hospital-physician sector became more price competitive, the rest of the industry experienced more real growth than the previously dominant sector, 8.7 to 7.3 percent real growth from 1985 to 2003. Such a high level of real growth in both sectors in this country, as well as in other developed countries, suggests that health services and products are highly valued by consumers, even without structural advantages that had been achieved in this country through provider domination of the health market.

Although the relationship between the two sectors of the health industry is complex, until recently hospitals, doctors, and physician-owned ambulatory care facilities were subject to much less price competition than dentists, nursing homes, home health agencies, and pharmaceutical concerns at all stages of the production and distribution processes. Insurance coverage has been much lower for the products and services provided by the other sector, as measured by the two columns reporting the percentage of expenditures made directly by consumers in Table 2.1. On both sides of the health care market the structural advantages surrounding health insurance and the consumer's freedom to choose any provider made it easier for hospitals and doctors to market their services independently of price considerations. Whether these advantages are responsible for the 1.5 percent average annual differential in growth from 1960 to 1985 is indeterminate, but this magnitude of difference is about 30 percent higher than the rate of other services.

Manning et al [1987] conclude from the Rand Health Insurance Experiment that health insurance coverage only explains about one-tenth of the real increase in health spending from 1950 to 1984. In contrast, the impact of producer dominance, as measured by the difference in the real rate of spending between the two sectors, approximates the excess share of gross domestic product (GDP) spent on health care by the United States over other developed nations. If the health industry had grown at the lower rate achieved in the other health sector over this 35-year period, total health spending in the United States would have been fifth highest level of spending among developed nations in 1985, 7.8 percent of the U.S. GDP. Instead, the United States actually spent 10.2 percent of its GDP on health care in 1985, or a 24 percent higher share.

In fact, a comparison of the way in which the U.S. health system operates in contrast to other developed nations provides additional evidence of producer dominance in the U.S. market. Drake's [1994] historical study of the U.S. health care market included an international comparison of health care systems in seven developed nations during the 1980s, which concluded that:

> The primary reason for higher hospital costs in the United States
> is precisely the same reason that U.S. physicians costs are so much
> higher—hospital and doctor services in the United States have

adopted an extremely intense, high tech, specialized style of care. The overinvestment in health care reflects the choice of technology that the United States has made and the comprehensiveness with which technology has been applied [Drake, 141].

Other Evidence of Provider Dominance

The managed care experience of the 1990s almost produced a stage of development unlike any previously experienced. That experience demonstrated that unilateral pricing practices, like the rates charged for new procedures, could have been eradicated in the competitive market that ended provider domination. Only since 1985, as competition in the rest of the economy made it harder for employers to pass their cost increases along to consumers, did employers finally make the effort to obtain price concessions from health care providers and control utilization of high-cost services to a sufficient extent to establish some price competition among providers.

That master stroke, which is taken for granted in other markets, is called "managed care", but is more accurately described as selective contracting. The employer or the firm's agent, usually an insurance company, gets bids on the price of care from various providers and then selects the low bidders, with a group of fee-for-service providers—called a preferred provider organization (PPO)—or with a comprehensive health care delivery and financing organization or brokered arrangement—called a health maintenance organization (HMO). And to encourage the employees to join the lower cost "managed care" plans, the employers have either limited consumer choice or structured the employees' choices by raising the out-of-pocket and premium sharing costs of the traditional fee-for-service comprehensive benefit plans and offered additional benefits, like prescription drugs, in the managed care plans.

Managed care was successful in reducing the rate of cost increases in much of the '90s. Health care spending increased much more rapidly than spending in the rest of the American economy for most of the century. Health spending constituted 5.2 percent of Gross Domestic Product (GDP) in 1960, 7.4 percent in 1970, 9.2 percent in 1980, and

12.2 percent in 1990, which means that over 30 years health spending was still growing more than twice as fast as the overall economy. After 1990 the health spending pace slowed. From 1993 through 1998, when health spending reached 13.7 percent of GDP, health spending ceased to grow any faster than the economy as a whole. In that six-year period, enrollment in managed care organizations rose from 54 percent of insured employees to 86 percent in 1998 [Levit et al, 2000].

A single change in the employer-based insurance mechanism, reducing the choice of providers and placing restrictions on utilization of some services, brought some price competition to the health care industry for the first time since World War II. Instead of permitting employees to have a "free" choice of provider, employers made them pay for choice or restructured the insurance benefit to provide employees with the promise of relatively lower out-of-pocket costs if they would restrict their utilization of health services to selected providers willing to negotiate the price of services and to accept either capitation payment or direct utilization controls.

Interestingly enough, the price competition that had been introduced by managed care has been directed primarily at hospital and doctors who commanded the lion's share (together, more than 65 to 70 percent) of health expenditures in the noncompetitive era after 1965. Their combined share, after reaching more than 71 percent in 1985, declined throughout the '90s and approached 65 percent of the total expenditures in 2000, but began to climb again in 2003. In a continuing pattern of unintended consequences for health care cost containment campaigns, the new villain—the fastest rising component—in the health sector is prescription drugs. Insurance for these drugs was added by the managed care organizations as an inducement for giving up free choice of physician and as a substitute for hospital and physician services. However, the inability to control drug prices represents the latest chapter in the failure to understand the expansionary effect of low deductibles on consumer behavior.

As a consequence, still another political problem has resulted: the Medicare program did not have a pharmaceutical benefit. While employed, many had drug benefits that insulated them against increased drug prices. However, these same individuals, now older, pay for their prescriptions at a time when many have chronic ailments requiring prescription drugs. The picture of poor older Americans who must choose between eating or filling their prescriptions was so compelling that both political parties scrambled to develop proposals for adding a prescription drug benefit to the Medicare program. In 2003, a drug benefit was added to the program, effective in 2006. The cycle of first dollar insurance benefits marches on: low-deductible insurance increases prices and utilization of services that inevitably lead to more insurance and still higher health care costs. The design of the drug benefit had one significant competitive feature—insurance carriers were required to compete on the basis of price for consumers and the insurers, in turn, negotiated with drug manufacturers. That competitive feature may offset the inflationary effect of first dollar coverage, but the overall result on cost remains unknown early in 2006.

Other changes in managed care have reduced price competition in the health care market. Employees have raised objections to these constraints on their consumption of health services. The so called "Patient Rights" legislative proposals seek to eliminate most of the restrictions on consumer behavior that have permitted buyers to negotiate with providers. As a result of these and other efforts, the bargaining advantages that insurers had in the '90s in negotiating prices with health care providers were gradually whittled away. As Ginsburg [2005] pointed out:

> Employers loosened many of the dimensions of managed care. They provided more preferred provider organization (PPO) options. They insisted on broader provider networks. They dropped authorization requirements to admit patients to hospitals, refer to specialists, or order expensive diagnostic or therapeutic procedures. They introduced HMO products that permitted access to specialists with a primary care referral [Ginsburg, 1516].

Needless to say, the result of liberalizing managed care is to drive health care price inflation back to double-digit rates of increase and restore the producer dominance by doctors and hospitals.

Politically, it is not surprising that individuals, given such a free ride for so long by the employers' provision of low deductible health insurance with free choice of provider, would resent the managed care limitations. If the United States is ever to gain competitive controls over the costs of health services, consumers must accept some responsibility for their economic behavior. Restoring markets after the prolonged absence of price competition will be extremely difficult. Proponents of a universal health insurance (UHI) plan believe that it can be used to provide sufficient inducements to consumers to encourage prudent behavior in purchasing health services and consumer concern about medical care prices. It is the lack of such concern that has caused Americans to have to pay the highest prices in the world for their health care. No amount of tinkering with the health care market is likely to overcome the deficiency in market competition in the health care industry.

Reconciliation with the Technology Explanation

Many health economists believe that technological change in the production of health services is the primary reason for health care spending rising faster than spending on other goods and services in the economy [Fuchs 1996]. If the cost of technological change is measured as the residual factor in the production of health services after accounting for increases in the quantity and cost of inputs, then more than half of health cost increases can be attributed to changes in medical technology—new services and new ways of providing existing services [Newhouse 1993]. Because growth in medical knowledge is largely determined by factors outside the market for health care services, many observers seem to assume that technology change is beyond market control.

The problem with the technology thesis for explaining higher health spending is that medical knowledge in the rest of the developed world is approximately the same as in the United States. The U.S. penchant for spending more on technology in health care can be explained both in terms of providing more invasive high-cost services, like organ transplants, to a larger number of patients than in other developed nations, but also because of the flawed market that gave substantial benefits to doctors and hospitals from higher U.S. investment in technology. In competitive markets profit determines when changes in knowledge are sufficient to revise methods of providing services or to provide new more efficacious services. In those markets new products are not introduced until consumers are willing to pay a price higher than the product's cost. And producers will not initiate new methods of production until cost savings are demonstrated.

However, in the producer-dominated health market hospital and physician profits could drive the introduction of new technologies even though consumers might not have been willing to pay for the new services or new production techniques under price-competitive supply and demand conditions. Few market controls have inhibited the direct application of new medical knowledge to new services and new ways of producing services. For example, introducing new technologies before understanding their costs and benefits has been only one way in which the innovative tendency has increased health care costs. Electronic fetal monitoring is a classic example of a technology that was introduced without any understanding of the benefits to be derived from the information it provided on fetal development. Nevertheless, it was quickly accepted in the mid-1960s as an integral part of obstetric medical practice even though it proved to have little or no effect on perinatal mortality and very limited evidence of benefit on perinatal morbidity [Banta and Thacker 1979].

One of the more costly problems has been the failure to discard obsolete products and production technologies when their lack of efficacy was widely understood by the medical profession. Tonsillectomy, with or without adenoidectomy, is a prime example of a product that medical science developed in the 1920s, which after the discovery of antibiotics proved not to be needed for most children with sore throats [Paradise et al 1984]. Children, primarily because of tonsillectomies, had the second largest admission rate of any age group in the 1930s, and their hospital utilization together with the rising number of births that took place in the hospital were the most significant sources of middle-class identification with the growing community hospital [Stevens 1989, 174]. Despite mounting evidence of the inappropriateness of this therapy for most children, T and As continued to be a substantial source of hospital admissions until the 1960s and beyond in some communities [Wennberg 1984]. The Paradise study took 11 years to demonstrate that few children needed this surgical procedure because of the difficulty in finding a suitable number of candidates who met the treatment protocol, only about 10 percent of the candidates recommended for T and As.

A trademark of the health care industry has been to operate new technologies alongside old ones that in other industries they would replace. For example, Showstack et al [1982] in a study of medical practice in a teaching hospital found that diagnostic procedures resulting from newly introduced technologies rose rapidly until a utilization plateau was reached, but that the old diagnostic procedures continued at the previously established rates of utilization. Another glitch in the producer-dominated market has been the ability of some physicians to earn excess profits from the introduction of new medical technologies. Roe [1981] described the failure of the medical market-place to adjust the pricing of new procedures after the procedure had attained general acceptance. A new procedure often is priced artificially high when it is introduced and volume is low. In other markets prices of new goods or services fall as sales increase. In health care, however, the high introductory price has often stuck, and some physicians earned exorbitant returns on these new procedures. The promise of such high returns has obviously encouraged medical innovation, but the rate and kind of innovation should change in a price competitive market.

Without price competition and the incentive to control costs, the health care industry has somehow managed to avoid innovating any significant new cost saving technologies, which is further proof it's hospital/physician dominance that is driving the kinds of technological innovations in the health care industry. During the 1990s, American companies in the competitive business sector made significant productivity gains (and thus cost savings) by computerizing their operations, but the health care industry did little in the way of computerizing their operations. Only the Veterans Administration has seriously invested in computerization of its health care programs and the payoff has been remarkable—the VA health care system went from being the worst to the best system of health care in the United States [Longman]. Even so, the federal government has been unsuccessful in getting the industry to develop a patient standardized computerized medical record, the heart of the VA system. New cost-saving technologies are available. For example, Steve Case, the founder of AOL and the previous chairman of Time Warner, has founded a company to modernize health records and information in a user friendly way that could assist physicians in providing better, safer care and consumers in purchasing health insurance and specific health care services [Clark]. There is no doubt that computers can be utilized to provide substantial improvements in quality and cost savings, if doctors, hospitals, and insurers will cooperate instead of blocking technologies that they feel may cramp the style of medicine that they wish to practice. Competitive markets can compel physicians to cooperate and implement quality-enhancement and cost-saving technologies to their own advantage.

The fundamental problem with producer domination is that it saps the discipline out of the market and replaces it with dependence on the producers' utility function. That's the major explanation for the United States having the most high-tech specialized form of care in the world. Whatever the producers wanted, within peer-accepted reason, could easily be accomplished without the normal resistance of buyer's price sensitivity; i.e., in the post-war period physicians started doing what they wanted to do, and they continued in ever greater numbers when they encountered no resistance. Individual physicians could choose a specialty based on their personal goals, without earnings in the more popular specialties declining to reflect a surplus number of practitioners. A surgeon could charge an absurdly high price for a new procedure solely to demonstrate the surgeon's professional prominence. Earning a good living from medicine was so easy that physicians' market decisions could emphasize non-economic considerations, such as professional prestige or personal satisfaction. However, physician behavior did not occur in a vacuum. Hospitals also benefited from the producer dominance. Hospital examples include the Robinson-Luft thesis of hospitals competing by increasing services and the investor-owned systems of hospitals that were established in the late 1960s and effortlessly earned abnormal profits by competing with not-for-profit hospitals whose cost standards were lax in an industry without price competition.

THE MARKET-DRIVEN UHI SYSTEM

Now with an understanding of the market defects in the health care industry, we can begin discussion of a UHI proposal that seeks to correct these defects. The prototype market-driven health insurance proposal was originally proposed in 1971 by Harvard economics professor Martin Feldstein [Eilers and Moyerman 1971], who recommended that the federal government provide last-dollar (or catastrophic) coverage to all citizens and also provide a government-guaranteed program of post-care loans to assist in financing the deductible and co-payment provisions of the coverage. Feldstein suggested that the deductible be established at 5 percent of family income followed by a 50 percent copayment on the next 10 percent of family income; i.e., the total health expenditures could be no higher than 10 percent of family income, but they would receive a federal benefit of 50 percent of health expenditures after spending 5 percent of their income. He recommended an exception for members below the federally-defined poverty of income, who should be eligible for first dollar (or zero deductible) of health care spending. Feldstein called his proposal an income-related catastrophic coverage, with the role of the federal government being insurer of last resort for all Americans and as guarantor for all health-caused loans required in financing the personal portion of health care expenditures.

The Feldstein proposal later was indirectly the subject of the largest study of consumer health spending in the Rand Health Insurance Experiment of the 1970s and '80s, directed by Professor Joseph

Newhouse, also of Harvard University. The project was funded by the Department of Health, Education, and Welfare to conduct a social experiment to understand the effects of cost sharing and health maintenance organizations by examining the behavior of 5,809 people in six sites around the country. Participants were randomly assigned to either a free care (a first-dollar insurance coverage) or, initially to one of four cost-sharing insurance plans for a three to five year period. The cost-sharing insurance plans all had a $1,000 limit on annual family out-of-pocket expenditures for nonpoor families. Poor families had an income-related limit to their out-of-pocket expenditures. Because of the Rand Experiment, we have considerable information and a better understanding of how consumer cost sharing affects the consumption of health care services and its effects on the health condition of the families studied [Newhouse et al 1993]. It provides much of the empirical data necessary for evaluating the income-related catastrophic UHI proposal. Although Professor Feldstein did not continue to actively support his health insurance proposal, the author made some additional refinements and amendments to the Feldstein proposal. It is the Drake proposal [1994] that will be outlined in this chapter and Appendix A, at the end of this chapter, contains an outline of legislation to implement this UHI plan.

Designing a Price-Competitive Health Plan

Advocates of a market-driven universal health insurance system begin with two objectives: (1) to correct the health insurance market for its failures as outlined earlier in this chapter; and, (2) to eliminate the inequities in access to health care that currently exist. In this section, the means of accomplishing the first goal will be discussed.

The U.S. health care market went astray because illness is not randomly distributed across the population. Most Americans are quite healthy and have relatively low total health care costs over their entire lives. Only a small portion of the total population will have serious illnesses and incur substantial health care costs. The key to designing a price-competitive health plan is to start over and address the actuaries' original two concerns about adverse selection and moral hazard in the insurance market. The simplest way of eliminating adverse selection (persons with the higher level of health care illnesses purchasing health insurance while healthier individuals do not) from the private health insurance market is to give the responsibility for insuring catastrophic illness to the federal government through a universal health insurance (UHI) program. Such a program represents an extension of the belief that a responsibility of government is to protect its citizens from risks beyond their control, such as temporary unemployment or natural disasters.

Unlike federal insurance against natural disasters or unemployment, however, the benefits of catastrophic illness insurance should be defined in terms of the cost of illness beyond the financial capability of a family to pay for necessary and appropriate care. That is, some expenditure for care is expected and affordable, while others are not. The cost of a $50,000 open-heart surgical procedure may be affordable to a millionaire or even a family earning $250,000 a year, but such surgery is totally beyond the financial capability of the nation's median-level family earning $45,000. The federal government should accept responsibility for insuring the cost of health care beyond whatever percent of a family's income that could reasonably be expected to be available for health care expenditures, probably between 10 and 20 percent. The government should also provide guaranteed loans to permit families to finance their share of the cost of care over time in a manner less disruptive of their life style.

For families earning below the federally-defined poverty level of income, few or no health care expenditures are affordable and families should be eligible for the first dollar of health care spending. Just getting to the care sites can be a major cost to families living in poverty. Perhaps for families whose income is approaching the poverty level, the percentage of income for the deductible should be less than the deductible for higher income families. Such a provision reduces the incentive for individuals whose income is close to the poverty line to stop working; work should always raise income. The specifics of legislation for catastrophic health insurance are beyond the scope of this book [see Feldstein, and Drake, 169-194] and will depend on actuarial cost studies for different benefit schedules and the budget assessment of what federal government resources are available to finance the program. However, one source of financing that should be included is changes in the income tax code: both the elimination of health spending deductions and the additional income tax revenues that could be derived by eliminating the tax exempt status of employer contributions for health insurance benefits, which encourages lower dollar-deductible insurance coverage than is optimal for a competitive market.

An income-related catastrophic health insurance program could be developed to correct the two structural deficiencies in the health insurance market. By making the federal government responsible for catastrophic insurance, private health insurers would no longer be driven by the concerns about adverse selection and individuals wanting additional coverage would be able to obtain it. In fact, coverage should be easier to obtain and cost less for lower income than the wealthier Americans because the lower-income person's dollar risk would be lower. Regardless of income, however, private health insurance premiums for benefits comparable to current levels should be at least a third lower with the government assuming the catastrophic illness liability. This premium saving more than offsets the new tax on employee health benefits for all but the highest income groups.

The problem of excess utilization of health care services by the catastrophically ill cannot be handled exclusively in the marketplace, however, and a variety of approaches will be required to find the best solutions. Each state should develop a plan for monitoring and controlling the health care costs of the catastrophically ill. Special program incentives may be developed for health care providers to find innovative programs for caring for these patients, such as the chronically ill receiving first dollar coverage being required to join an HMO that provides specialized care in that particular chronic disease and the federal government should split its savings in catastrophic expenses for specialized health care delivery organizations that find effective means for reducing the costs of caring for chronic ill patients. Alternatively, regulation and/or rationing of particular treatment regimens may be required. Although there are no guaranteed solutions, experimentation and a focus on the appropriateness of treatment for these patients may lead to better and more economical care. Under the current insurance schemes, these patients are avoided, not singled out for special attention in efficaciously meeting their health needs.

In addition to eliminating the effect of adverse selection in the health insurance market, a more significant advantage of catastrophic coverage is to minimize the effect of moral hazard on the utilization of health services. Families would have appropriate incentives to be prudent in purchasing care. While there would be no financial barrier for getting care that a family and its medical advisors believed necessary, the family would have an incentive to investigate costs of alternative treatment plans and providers. Consumers cannot play a significant or decisive role in the health care market without directly assuming their affordable share of the financial responsibility for the purchase of health care services. And the third flaw in the current market, lack of a consumer advisory agent, would be corrected by adding a new private organization for administering the catastrophic insurance plan. An agency is needed to certify that health care expenditures did qualify for the deductible limits of the catastrophic benefits, and to ensure that all consumers, both the employed and unemployed, receive all eligible federal benefits and that they, in turn, pay their deductible for health services.

This new private agency, called the Health Care Financing Agency (HCFA), could become, at long last, the consumer's independent agent or broker in buying health services and would be accredited and supervised by the Department of Health and Human Services. Annually, each family would choose its HCFA from among those private organizations in the geographic area that have been accredited by HHS to serve this role. The cost of operating the HCFAs should be split between the government for monitoring health care spending and the consumer for providing information about and negotiating prices of health care services. It is especially important to have the consumers involved in purchasing HCFA services to establish a new master-agent relationship and correct the failure of health insurance companies to view consumers as clients.

In competing for enrollees, the consumer assistance agencies could offer a number of additional services such as: (1) perform the function of negotiating prices with health care providers and/or assuming a specific risk function below the catastrophic limits; (2) integrate health care delivery and financing as HMOs do; or (3) perform multiple financing/information functions for consumers who wish to self-insure for the deductible, but want to obtain information about fee-for-service providers (pricing as well as professional credentials) and/or treatment options by making available panels of professional experts to provide consumers with medical advice.

In other words, these organizations could perform all of the functions currently being performed by different types of health insurance companies in today's market, but their new client would be the consumer. Because the consumer has never had an independent advisor in making health care consumption decisions, the competition between health care providers, traditional health insurers, PPOs, HMOs, new finance and information service organizations to serve consumers ought to be extremely productive.

Consumer Responsibilities and Benefits
The kinds of health care service and financing choices that will be made available to consumers should much more closely approximate the range of options routinely expected in other U.S. consumer markets. This reform proposal is directed almost exclusively to changes on the demand side of the health care market. There is no assumption that a particular organization of health care services is optimal for all consumers. In fact, greater specialization (in the economic rather than medical sense) in the marketplace can be expected with different forms of organization seeking to achieve lower costs for treating various illnesses and even greater incentives for the division of organized care into primary and specialist components.

The financing and health information advisory agency should enhance the consumer's ability to purchase services in the fee-for-service, a la carte, part of the delivery system. By collecting and making available market information about prices and medical outcomes, the consumer who only infrequently buys services has an opportunity to become sensitive to and knowledgeable about price and quality of competing fee-for-service providers.

Speculation about how health care providers will respond to this more cost sensitive and knowledgeable consumer can be illustrated by thinking about the HMO in a reformed market. First, HMO enrollees in such a market are likely to be less healthy than the consumers in the fee-for-service part of the health care system as the 1930s actuaries predicted. Healthier consumers are much more likely to self-insure for their deductible, and those consumers with either chronic illness or in an acute episode of illness, now subject to buying insurance for or directly paying the deductible, will be drawn to the HMO's lower out-of-pocket fees or health care organizations specializing in treatment of particular illnesses. Because the growth market for these organizations will be among the sicker members of society, the integrated delivery organizations will be challenged to find less expensive ways of treating particular disease entities and could also be organized differently.

An integrated delivery organization could consist of a large primary care group practice that provides the health education and preventive services, as well as the primary diagnostic and therapeutic care, and then buys specialist and institutional care as needed across a broad spectrum of the market, giving their enrollees greater choice of specialists and hospitals. The capital needs for the insurance risk will be reduced significantly because the catastrophic coverage acts like a family-based stop-loss insurance to providers, who can look to the federal government for coverage after the family has incurred expenses exceeding its deductible.

Concerns have been raised about the compatibility of markets with health care services. Currently, much lower levels of tension between buyers and sellers exist in the health care market than in other markets. Having lower consumer tension in the purchase of health care services may have some benefits. Victor Fuchs, a leading health economist, has identified a number of reasons for lower market tension in health care. He cites imperfect knowledge on the part of the consumer, a highly personal and intimate relationship between patients and physicians, a production function (the healing process) that uniquely requires patients and health professionals to work cooperatively to establish mutual trust and confidence rather than the normal adversarial relationship between buyers and sellers, and the necessary, emotional decisions of dealing with dying and death that "can leave a lifelong residue of guilt and regret" as reasons for diminishing the role of a bargain-hunting consumer in health care markets. The consumer's HCFA could also assist in providing information about alternative treatment regimens

Although this market reform proposal does seek to create some market tension in the purchase of health care services, it also seeks to ensure that all Americans can afford all needed health care services by assisting in the financing of affordable (based on family income) services through loan guarantees and by making it government's responsibility to pay for all unaffordable services, the catastrophic coverage. It does, indeed, reward and penalize health care consumers for the economic appropriateness of their behavior. The demand for health insurance will reflect the tension that arises from the recognition that more spent on health care means less will be available for other goods and services. However, the focus of this tension is on the financing decisions about coverage below the federal deductible—all Americans need to make that decision in a prudent manner—with minimal market tension when health services are delivered.

Fortunately, Americans rarely have to make many difficult decisions about care alternatives, or are faced with life and death problems concerning themselves or their loved ones. Hiatt [1975] argues that it is widespread misconception that the principal objective of medical practice is the prevention of death, and he cites a study by Bunker [1974], which points out that "only a small fraction of surgery and a smaller fraction of nonsurgical encounters involved life-and-death decisions [while] most are directed at the provision of relief from physical or emotional discomfort or disability."

The separation of the insurance-financing decision from those care decisions, coupled with a guarantee to all Americans of financial and advisory assistance in the purchase of needed health care services, should provide safeguards for the special working relationship between patients and their chosen physicians to build trust and cooperation in the healing process that Fuchs has properly argued is essential to the design of an effective health care market.

The current insurance mechanism limits consumer choice to the selection of health care providers, with either a defined group or all providers, and perhaps a third option for the defined group of paying more to see providers outside that group. However, most all employees are expected to buy insurance for a low-dollar comprehensive set of services. The system does not encourage consumers to prepay for a bundle of specific services that are designed for an individual's specific health care needs. During the life cycle from youth, to marriage, to child-rearing, to middle and old age, the kind of available health insurance benefits are the same even though most service needs are quite predictably different. Why are all packages identical when the actual needs are very idiosyncratic? The reformed market must give a broader range of choice of benefits to permit consumers to tailor their prepayment of services to those particular items that they expect to need, and to depend on general insurance coverage for their unexpected needs. A universal program of income-related catastrophic health insurance coverage, paid for out of taxes on the employee's current health benefits, can correct the major shortcomings in the health care market without continuing the adversarial relationship between buyers and sellers that has developed in managed care programs. All Americans can have access to necessary information about needed health care services with confidence that the specific services provided have been designed to meet their needs and are being produced as efficiently as other goods and services in the remarkable American economy. If this level of performance is achieved, U.S. health services would truly be world-class.

THE SINGLE-PAYER NHI SYSTEM

Two Harvard Medical School professors, David U. Himmelstein, M.D. and Steffie Woolhandler, M.D., MPH, have led a group of dedicated physicians in espousing a governmentally operated national health insurance program, which would be financed primarily by payroll taxes and provide uniform benefits to all Americans without any co-payments or deductibles. Himmelstein and Woolhandler (H-W) co-founded the Physicians for a National Health Insurance Program (PNHIP) in 1986 to advance a proposal that is based on the Canadian health insurance system. The proposal was introduced into the House of Representatives during the 108th (2003-04) Congress by Democratic Representative John Conyers of Michigan, called the United States National Health Insurance Act (HR676) [See Appendix B at the end of this chapter]. Senator Edward Kennedy first introduced a single-payer national health insurance bill in 1970. Because the proposal is totally consistent with the concepts of social insurance, it, or something very similar, is likely to be the type of legislative proposal that will be introduced and supported by liberal Democratic legislators in future Congresses.

Antithesis of the Market Approach
Although the primary objective of the single payer approach is to achieve absolute equity among all Americans, a broader statement of the program includes four principles that shape the reform program:

1. Access to comprehensive health care is a human right. It is the responsibility of society, through its government, to ensure this right. Coverage should not be tied to employment.
2. The right to choose and change one's physician is fundamental to patient autonomy. Patients should be free to seek care from any licensed health care professional.
3. Pursuit of corporate profits and personal fortune have no place in caregiving. They create enormous waste and too often warp clinical decision making.
4. In a democracy, the public should set health policies and budgets. Personal medical decisions must be made by patients with their caregivers, not by corporate or government bureaucrats [The Physicians' Working Group for Single-Payer National Health Insurance].

Doctors H-W, both primary care physicians, want to ensure that all Americans, regardless of income, can have the same access to care and are not discouraged from seeking that care because of any economic limitations. Copayments and deductibles would be illegal under the proposal because they can act as deterrents to seeking care and could discourage prospective patients from receiving timely preventive care that will hasten cure or postpone illness or death.

H-W support the AMA's cherished goal of the freedom of choice of physician, but emphasize that the purpose of the principle is to respect the patient's right to choose. They also support all forms of practice—solo practice, group practice, and health maintenance organizations—and all forms of professional compensation—fee-for-service, salaried arrangements, and capitation payment. Patients would retain the right to make medical care decisions in conjunction with their selected personal caregivers.

Unlike advocates of market reform, Doctors Himmelstein and Woolhandler oppose any profit-seeking activity in the delivery of health care services. HR676, USNHI, provides for the buyout over 15 years of real estate, buildings, and equipment of for-profit health care enterprises by the U.S. government, which presumably would then operate the facilities or sell them to not-for-profit organizations to operate. Physicians, dentists, and other health care professionals, many of whom in a sense operate their practices as profit-seeking enterprises, could continue to operate on a fee-for-service basis, but the fees would be set by the U.S. National Health Insurance (USNHI) program. Physicians would be precluded from operating for-profit laboratories, surgicenters, or other ancillary patient service centers after the 15 year grace period for the buy-out of for-profit health care enterprises. The program would, however, permit drug manufacturers to continue to be profit-seeking corporations, but would have the federal government negotiate (establish) prices for prescription drugs and create a national formulary that would define acceptable prescription drugs and encourage best-practices. Private health insurers are legislatively prohibited from selling health insurance that in any way duplicates the benefits of the USNHI program, but they could sell insurance for cosmetic services.

The specific health insurance benefits of the program are not defined in the proposed legislation other than "all medically necessary services" including primary care and prevention, long term care, mental health services, the full scope of dental services (excluding cosmetic dentistry), as well as all the various institutional settings for acute care. Although it isn't spelled out, the set of benefits is likely to extend beyond Medicare benefits for long term care and mental health services, as well the dentistry benefit.

In place of the market determination of resource allocations, the program would designate the USNHI to allocate national health care funds to existing Medicare regions. The regional authorities would administer the program and allocate the region's share of funds through global budgets to hospitals, nursing homes, and other health care providers. Except for doctor and dentist's fees that are federally approved and the negotiated prices of prescription drugs, prices would virtually disappear in the health care system and a budget system of fiscal controls would be substituted. Although the proposed legislation is largely silent on the specific operation of the top-down allocations to the regional authorities and then to individual health care providers and organizations, the bill does contain provisions for a National Program Advisory Board and State (Program) Directors, appointed by the governor of each state, whose principal responsibility would be to oversee health care assessments and operate the health planning process, including the spending of the capital budget, which is separately funded from the operating budget.

Instead of the market determining the quantity of resources available for health care and allocating those funds throughout the system, a tax fund would determine how much would be available for health care. According to the executive summary of USNHI, that funding would be derived from:

A payroll tax on all employers of 3.3%. Maintain employee and employer Medicare payroll tax of 1.45%. Implement a variety of mechanisms so that low and middle income families pay a smaller share of their incomes for health care than wealthiest 5% of

Americans, a small tax on stock and bond transfers, and closing corporate tax shelter. A repeal of the Bush tax cut of 2001. For more details, see PHNP's Financing National Health Insurance" [Conyers and Appendix B].

The complete bill for USNHI is silent on the source of funding, except to say that there may be an annual appropriation of "such sums as may be necessary" and that "It is the intention of Congress that over time the Program is to be primarily funded through a progressive payroll tax and income taxes," presumably as exemplified in the bill's executive summary. Thus, for the vast majority of Americans, except for the wealthiest five percent, the amount of their spending on health care would be substantially reduced. Employers, the wealthiest five percent of Americans, and businesses would pay the bulk of the nation's health care expenses.

In addition, one of the primary arguments that proponents of single-payer NHI advance is that having a single payer for all of health care would drastically reduce administrative costs of the program, citing both the lower administrative cost ratio of Medicare in comparison for private health insurance and the Canadian health plan's lower administrative costs. Doctors H-W estimated that in 1999 the United States could have saved $209 billion in administration costs based on the Canadian system [Woolhander et al 2003]. Although economist Henry Aaron [2003] of the Brookings Institution in a review article, trimmed those savings to $159 billion, that still represents nearly 15 percent of personal health care expenditures in 1999. Those one-time savings would help significantly in designing a smaller tax package to finance the initial year of operation of the USNHI program that the United States would be spending at the time of program commencement and would contribute significantly to lowering the quantity of resources devoted to health care as a percentage of total output, reducing health care expenditures from 13.1 percent of GDP to 11.4 percent in 1999 by Aaron's slightly lower estimate of savings.

A Perfect Solution

The single-payer NHI proposal, at least on the surface, appears to be a perfect solution to America's health care problems. All Americans would be eligible to receive all "medically necessary health care" from caregivers of their choice. The costs of health care, after the elimination of all unnecessary administrative costs, would be capped by amount of tax funds that will be raised in accordance with the provisions of the legislation, but there would be the possibility of special supplementary appropriations by Congress for any unexpected health care needs beyond those financed through the designated tax sources. A hierarchical federal-regional-state system would regulate the quality of care, including the specification of a computerized diagnostic and outcome measurement system, to ensure that all Americans receive high quality care. Capital for new investment or maintenance of the health care delivery system would similarly be allocated through regional-state planning authorities to ensure that no investment would be wasteful or duplicative. The public would be represented on a national advisory board and through participation in the regional-state quality-review and planning functions, and expert professional opinions would be available in all of the regulatory processes.

The designers and advocates of the single-payer NHI seem to have responded to all of the major problems currently existing in the health care market. The only hesitation will be the natural reluctance Americans have traditionally shown about delegating too much responsibility to active government operations in the marketplace, especially because most Americans understand that the market economy has worked well in other sectors in providing for the economic health of the nation. Indeed, the economic performance of only two industries, both vital to the social and economic welfare of Americans, differs significantly from the general success of the rest of the American economy. The elementary and secondary education system in the United States has been unable to control costs or to satisfy the educational objectives for children and the nation's health care system has been unable to contain costs or provide for the equitable distribution of health care. These inferior results stem from the fact that neither service is produced under conditions of price competition as it exists in the rest of the economy. The efficiency problem in these two industries is not insignificant because together they constituted nearly 20 percent of the nation's GDP in 2005 (public education, 3.8 percent, and health, 16 percent). Market advocates believe that the federal government could correct both the efficiency and distributional problems by employing subsidy programs that utilize market-type incentives to create a more competitive environment, to the overall benefit of all Americans. The single-payer advocates believe that a market is inappropriate to the provision of health care, that it is wasteful and inhumane to subject the sick to the rigors of a marketplace mentality and that is immoral to make profits out of sickness.

The dispute between single-payer and market-driven advocates is not about the goals for a federal health insurance program for America, but it is about which method—markets or government—can best achieve those goals. All Americans want more equitable access of all Americans to health care that is produced in a cost-effective and efficacious manner. The unanswered question is: which method of providing health insurance to all Americans can best achieve that goal? That is the question that we will try to answer in the next two chapters by, first, examining the economics of the two proposals and then considering, in turn, the politics of enacting and operating the reformed American health care system.

BIBLIOGRAPHY

Aaron, H. "The costs of health care administration in the United States and Canada—Questionable answers to a questionable question," *New England Journal of Medicine*, Vol. 349, August 21, 2003, pp. 801-3.

Anderson, O.W., *Health Services in the United States: A Growth Enterprise Since 1875*, Ann Arbor, MI: Health Administration Press, 1985.

Banta, H.D., and Thacker, S.B., "Policies toward Medical Technology: The Case of Electronic Fetal Monitoring," *American Journal of Public Health*, Vol. 69, September 1979, pp. 931-935.

Bunker, J., "Risks and Benefits from Surgery." In, Taylor, D., ed., *From Benefits and Risks in Medical Care: A Symposium Held by the Office of Health Economics*, Luton, UK: White Crescent Press, Ltd., 1974.

Clark, K., "The Case for Healthcare," *U.S. News & World Reports*, October 17, 2005.

Conyers, J., "Executive Summary of The United States National Health Insurance Act (HR676)," http://www.pnhp.org/nhibill/nhi_exec.summ.html, February 3, 2003.

Dickinson, F.G., *A Brief History of the Attitude of the American Medical Association Toward Voluntary Health Insurance*, Bulletin 70, Chicago: American Medical Association, 1946.

Drake, D.F., *Reforming the Health Care Market: An Interpretive Economic History*, Washington, DC: Georgetown University Press, 1994.

Feldman, R., and Sloan, F., "Health Economics: A Report on the Field," *Journal of Health Politics, Policy and Law,* Vol. 15, No. 3 (Fall, 1990), pp. 627-47.

Feldstein, M.S., "The Feldstein Plan," in Ellers, R.D., and Moyerman, S.S., editors, *National Health Insurance, Proceedings of the Conference on National Health Insurance*, Homewood, IL: Richard D. Irwin, Inc. for the Leonard Davis Institute of Health Economics, 1971

Fisher, C.R., "Differences by Age Groups in Health Care Spending," *Health Care Financing Review*, Vol 1, No. 2 (Spring, 1980), pp. 65-90.

Freymann, J.G., *The American Health Care Systems: Its Genesis and Trajectory*, New York: Medcom, 1974.

Fuchs, V.R., "Economic, Values, and Health Care Reform," Presidential Address to the American Economic Association, 1996.

Ginsburg, P., "Competition in Health Care: Its Evolution over the Past Decade," *Health Affairs*, Vol. 24, No. 6 (November/December 2005), pp. 1512-1522.

Hiatt, H.H. "Protecting the Medical Commons: Who is Responsible?" *New England Journal of Medicine*, Vol. 293, July 31, 1975, pp. 235-241.

Lazenby, H.C., and Letsch, S.W., "National Health Expenditures, 1989," *Health Care Financing Review*, Vol. 12, No. 4 (Winter 1990), pp. 1-26.

Levit, K., Smith, C., Cowan, C., Lazenby, H., and Martin, A., "Inflation Spurs Health Spending in 2000," *Health Affairs*, Vol. 21, No. 1 (January/February 2002), pp. 172-181.

Levit, K.R., Cowan, C.A., Laxenby, H., et al, "Health Spending in 1998: Signals of Change," *Health Affairs,* Vol. 19, No. 1 (January/ February, 2000), pp. 124-132.

Levit, K.R., Lazenby, H.C., Braden, B.R., Cowan, C.A., McDonnell, P.A., Sivarajan, L., Stiller, J.M., Won, D.K., Donham, C.S., Long, A.M., and Stewart, M.S., "National Health Expenditures, 1995," *Health Care Financing Review*, Vol. 17, No. 3 (Fall 1996a), pp. 175-214.

Levit, K.R., Lazenby, H.C., Sivarajan, L., Stewart, M.W., Braden, B.R., Cowan, C.A., Donham, C.S., Long, A.M., McDonnell, P.A., Sensenig, A.L., Stiller, J.M., and Won, D.K., "National Health Expenditures, 1994," *Health Care Financing Review*, Vol. 17, No. 2 (Spring, 1996b), pp. 205-242.

Levit, K.R., Olin, G.L., and Letsch, S.W., "Americans' Health Insurance Coverage, 1980-91." *Health Care Financing Review*, Vol., 14, No. 1 (Fall 1992), pp. 31-57.

Levit, K.R., Lazenby, H.C., Waldo, D.R., and Davidoff, L.M., "National Health Expenditures, 1984," *Health Care Financing Review*, Vol. 7, No. 3 (Fall, 1985), pp. 1-35.

Longman, P. "The Best Care Anywhere," *Washington Monthly*, January/February 2005, http://www.washingtonmonthly.com/features/ 2005/0501.longman.html.

Manning, W.G., Newhouse, J.P., Duan, N., Keeler, E.B., Leibowitz, A., and Marquis, M.S., "Health Insurance and the Demand for Medical Care: Evidence from a Randomized Experiment," *American Economic Review*, Vol. 77, June, 1987, pp. 251-277.

McMillan, A., "Trends in Medicare Health Maintenance Organization Enrollment: 1986-93," *Health Care Financing Review*, Vol. 15, No. 4 (Fall 1993), pp. 135-146.

Newhouse, J.P., "The Structure of Health Insurance and the Erosion of Competition in the Medical Marketplace," in *Competition in the Health Sector: Past, Present, and Future,* ed. W. Greenburg, Germantown, MD: Aspen Systems, 1978.

"Has the Erosion of the Medical Marketplace Ended?" *Journal of Health Politics, Policy and Law*, Vol. 13, No. 3 (Summer 1988), pp. 263-278.

"An Iconoclastic View of Health Cost Containment," *Health Affairs*, Vol. 12 (Supplement 1993), pp. 172-193.

Newhouse, J.P., and the Insurance Experiment Group, *Free for All? Lessons from the Rand Health Insurance Experience Group*, Cambridge, MA: Harvard University Press, 1993.

Paradise, J.L., Bluestone, C.D., Bachman, R.Z., et al, "Efficiency of Tonsillectomy for Recurrent Throat Infections in Severely Affected Children," *New England Journal of Medicine*, Vol. 310, March 15, 1984, pp. 674-683.

The Physicians' Working Group for Single-Payer National Health Insurance (Woolhandler, S., Himmelstein, D.U., Angeli, M, and Young, Q.D.), "Proposal of the Physicians' Working Group for Single-Payer National Health Insurance," *Journal of American Medical Association*, Vol. 290, No. 6 (August 13, 2003), pp. 798-805.

Robinson, J.C., and Luft, H.S., "Competition and the Cost of Hospital Care, 1972-1982." *Journal of American Medical Association*, Vol. 257, June 19, 1987, pp. 3241-3245.

Roe, B.B., "The UCR Boondoggle: A Death Knell for Private Practice," *New England Journal of Medicine*, Vol. 305, July 2, 1981, pp. 41-15.

Showstack, J.A., Schroeder, S.A., Matsumoto, M.F., "Changes in the Use of Medical Technologies," *New England Journal of Medicine*, Vol. 306, March 25, 1982, pp. 706-712.

Smith, C., Cowan, C., Heffler, S., Catlin, A., and the National Health Accounts Team, "National Health Spending in 2004: Recent Slowdown Led by Prescription Drugs," *Health Affairs*, Vol. 25, No. 1 (January/February 2006), pp. 186-196.

Stevens, R. *In Sickness and in Wealth: American Hospitals in the Twentieth Century*, New York: Basic Books, Inc., 1989.

U.S. Department of Health and Human Services, *Health Care Financing Review: Medicare and Medicaid Statistical Supplement, 1995*, Washington, DC: U.S. Government Printing Office, 1995.

Waldo, D.R., Sonnefeld, S.T., McKusick, D.R., and Arnett, R.H., "Health expenditures by age group, 1977 and 1987." *Health Care Financing Review*, Vol. 10, No. 4 (Summer 1989), pp. 111-121, and an Errata. *Ibid.*, Vol. 11, No. 1 (Fall 1989), pp. 165-167.

Wennberg, J., "Dealing with Medical Practice Variations: A Proposal for Action," *Health Affairs*, Vol. 3 (Summer, 1984), pp. 6-33.

Woolhandler, S. Campbell, X., and Himmelstein, D.U., "Costs of Health Administration in the United States and Canada, *New England Journal of Medicine*, Vol. 349, August 21, 2003, pp. 768-775.

APPENDIX A

The Affordable Health Care Reform, Universal Health Insurance, and Employment Revitalization Act*

Purposes

1. To initiate fundamental reform of the nation's health care financing and delivery system by:

    A.   providing financial assistance by the federal government to all citizens and alien residents, in accordance with the person's ability to pay, for the purchase of health care services; and

    B.   containing health care costs through a restructuring of private health insurance to limit consumers' liability according to family income and to eliminate the risk of catastrophic illness from health insurance carriers and comprehensive health care delivery organizations.

2. To encourage the employment of additional full-time employees and to stimulate economic growth by:

    A.   limiting the employer's obligation for employees health insurance benefits to existing levels and reducing their obligations for retired employees health benefits; and,

*Adopted from D.F. Drake, *Reforming the Health Care Market: An Interpretive Economic History*, Washington, DC: Georgetown University Press, 1994.

B.   providing incentives for economic growth to American businesses by lowering fixed labor costs and reducing their retirement liabilities and to consumers by providing a portable set of building-block health insurance benefits and, in the transition, making it possible to increase their aggregate net cash wages.

3. To accomplish the first two objectives without either increasing the national debt or risking the future of the nation's health care delivery system on a single, untried method of organizing and health care system by:

A.   limiting the federal government's obligation for financing health care services to the aged and disabled, through an enriched Medicare program, and persons whose family income is below 200 percent of the poverty level or who are catastrophically ill and by raising tax revenues necessary for the full financing of program costs through means that are either progressive or will promote healthier lifestyles; and,

B.   requiring state administration of the program to ensure systematic experimentation with alternative methods of controlling and organizing health care delivery.

Health Care Benefits

1. The definition of health care services that will qualify for federal financial assistance are the benefits described in the American Health Security Act [Clinton's proposed health insurance legislation of 1993] with some modification of the deductibles and copayments according to family income. Persons who are aged 65 and over or are classified as permanently disabled at the time this act goes into operation shall continue to be eligible for Medicare benefits for the remainder of their lives.

2. The amount of direct federal assistance available to any individual will be determined by the individual's family income and the excess of expenditures for these comprehensive health care services made by the individual or family over a deductible of 5 percent of that family income plus copayments of 50 percent of an additional 10 [or 20] percent of the family income for all citizens whose income is below 200 percent of the poverty level, and individuals entitled to Medicare benefits. The lower-income families shall be eligible for federal assistance without any deductible or copayment. Medicare beneficiaries, eligible prior to October 1, 2010, shall retain their their existing benefits, but beneficiaries becoming entitled after September 30, 2010, except for low-income families, shall be limited to a deductible, based on personal out-of-pocket expenditures, of 10 [or 20] percent of family income.

3. In addition to direct federal assistance, the federal government will establish a loan guarantee program for assisting individuals in obtaining postcare financing through Health Care Financing Agencies for their out-of-pocket health care service costs. The federal government, through the Internal Revenue Service, will assist the financing agencies in the collection of those obligations that become past due.

Financing Federal Program Costs

1. The primary source of financing the program costs will be through amendment of the Internal Revenue Code to eliminate tax deductions of health spending and redefine taxable income for individuals to include payments made by employers for health insurance premiums on the individual's behalf. [See the section of Program Transition for an employee option to convert employer health premiums into cash salaries.]

2. The secondary source of financing will be the same increases in the so-called "sin" taxes on tobacco that are included in the American Health Security Act.

3. During the first five years of the program's operation, a third source of financing will be payments from state governments in amounts initially equal to their Medicaid expenditures in the year prior to program implementation. These payments will decline by at least 20 percent in each of the first five years of the program and the rate of decline may increase even more rapidly if the National Health Board concludes that a particular state's performance in meeting its responsibilities for administering the federal program produces superior reduction in the state's rate of health care inflation.

Program Administration

1. Overall direction for the administration of the program will be the responsibility of the National Health Board similar to the body included in the American Health Security Act except that this body will be limited to overseeing and evaluating the program and monitoring the state program performance; approving different types of state experiments with health care financing and regulation; and periodically reporting on the health insurance programs operation to the Congress and recommending legislative changes, when appropriate.

2. Each state would be required to establish an authority for administering the federal program in accordance with federal standards established in the legislation. In addition to ensuring that each U.S. citizen and resident alien receives the catastrophic health insurance benefit and that HMO registration for low-income beneficiaries suffering from chronic illness is competitively bid and low-income beneficiaries are assigned to convenient and accessible HMOs, these standards include a plan for expanding primary care in the state, a plan for the management of care for the catastrophically ill—including the federal government's willingness to share savings with organizations that develop cost-effective, disease-specific care programs, and a program for approving and monitoring Health Care Financing Agencies that ensure that each citizen has a choice of agencies for receiving all his/her benefits from the federal assistance program and certifies the

agency's competence to provide other financing, advisory, or health services. If the state cannot develop a satisfactory plan or subsequently does not make sufficient progress in accomplishing its goals, then the federal government would be required to administer an appropriate plan for that state.

3. Health Care Financing Agencies will be responsible for ensuring that all residents receive benefits for federal assistance, arranging postcare loans for obligations citizens incur in purchasing qualified health care services, and can offer other services as certified by the state health agency to assist residents with the financing and consumption of health care services.

Program Operation and Transition

1. In the year of implementation each employee receiving employer-purchased health insurance would have the option of either directing the employer to pay an amount equal to all or part of the previous year's premium to his/her designated Health Care Financing Agency, or to have the employer increase his/her wages by all or part of that last year's premium. However, the employer's future obligation for employee health benefits would be fixed at whatever dollar amount the employee designates in the year of implementation unless the employer agrees to increase the contribution in future wage negotiations. All employers are, however, obligated to make available to all employees the opportunity to purchase health insurance and offer several insurance options as defined by the National Health Board.

2. The legislation would include a plan detailing the time schedule for establishing the National Health Board, the development and approval of state health plans, the mechanism for exercising the individual's choice of Health Care Financing Agency, and the employee's direction to his/her employer of either premium designation or increased wages.

APPENDIX B

Executive Summary of
The United States National Health Insurance Act
(HR676)
("Expanded & Improve Medicare for All Bill")
Introduced by Congressman John Conyers,
108ᵗʰ Congress*

Brief Summary of Legislation

The United States National Health Insurance Act (HR676) established a new American national health insurance program by creating a single payer health care system. The bill would create a publicly financed, privately delivered health care program that uses the already existing Medicare program by expanding and improving it to all U.S. residents, and all residents living in U.S. territories. The goal of the legislation is to ensure that all Americans, guaranteed by law, will have access to the highest quality and cost effective health care services regardless of one's employment, income, or health status.

With over 42 million uninsured Americans, and another 40 million who are under insured, the time has come to change our inefficient and costly fragmented health care system. The USNHI program would reduce overall annual health care spending by over $50 billion in the first year. In addition, because it implements effective methods of cost-control, health spending is contained over time, ensuring affordable health care to future generations.

*From http://www.phhp.org/nhibill/nhi_execsumm.html. For more information, contact Joel Segal, legislative assistant, Rep. John Conyers at 202 225-5126 or email at Joel.Segal @mail.house.gov.

In its first year, single-payer will save over $150 billion on paperwork and $50 billion by using rational bulk purchasing of medications. Those savings are more than enough to cover all the uninsured, improve coverage for everyone else, including medication coverage and long-term care.

Employers who currently provide coverage for employees pay an average of 8.5% of payroll towards health coverage, while many employers cannot coverage at all. Under this Act, all employers will pay a modest 3.3% payroll tax per employee, while eliminating their payments toward private health plans. The average cost to an employee earning $35,000 per year will be reduced to $1,155, less than $100 per month.

95% of families will pay less for health care under national insurance than they do today. Seniors and younger people will all have the comprehensive medication coverage they need.

Who Is Eligible

Every person living in the United States and the U.S. Territories would receive a United States National Health Insurance Card and i.d number once they enroll at the appropriate location. Social Security numbers may not be used when assigning i.d cards. No co-pays or deductibles are permissible under this act.

Benefits/Portability

This program will cover all medically necessary services, including primary care, inpatient care, outpatient care, emergency care, prescription drugs, durable medical equipment, long-term care, mental health services, dentistry, eye care, chiropractic, and substance abuse treatment. Patients have their choice of physicians, providers, hospitals, clinics, and practices.

Conversion to a Non-Profit Health Care System

Private health insurers shall be prohibited under this act from selling coverage that duplicates the benefits of the USNHI program. They shall not be prohibited from selling coverage for any additional benefits not covered this Act; examples include cosmetic surgery and other medically unnecessary treatments.

Cost Containment Provisions/Reimbursement

The National USNHI program will annually set reimbursement rates for physicians, health care providers, and negotiate prescription drug prices. The national office will provide annual lump sum allotment to each existing Medicare region, which will then administer the program. Payment to health care providers include fee for service, and global budgets.

The conversion to a not-for-profit health care system will take place over a 15 year period, through the sale of U.S. treasury bonds; payment will not be made for loss of business profits, but only for real estate, buildings, and equipment.

Funding & Administration

The United States Congress will establish annual funding outlays for the USNHI Program through an annual entitlement. The USNHI program will operate under the auspices of the Dept. of Health & Human Services, and be administered in the former Medicare offices. All current expenditures for public health insurance programs such as S-CHIP, Medicaid, and Medicare will be place into the USNHI program.

A National USNHI Advisory Board will be established, comprised of health care professionals and representatives of health advocacy groups.

Proposed Funding for USNHI Program: $1.86 Trillion Per Year

A payroll tax on all employers of 3.3%. Maintain employee and employer Medicare payroll tax of 1.45%. Implement a variety of mechanisms so that low and middle income families pay a smaller share of their incomes for health care than wealthiest 5% of Americans; i.e., a health income tax on the wealthiest 5% of Americans, a small tax on stock and bond transfers, and closing corporate tax shelters. A repeal of the Bush tax cut of 2001. For more details, see PNHP's "Financing National Health Insurance."

CHAPTER 3
Evaluating the Economic Effects of the Two Prototype Reforms

In this chapter, the economic attributes of the two reform proposals will be considered. Because the market-driven and single-payer reform proposals are so different, evaluating the economic effects of the two proposals requires different analyses. The market-driven system has to be evaluated in terms of how well it would eliminate the current health care market deficiencies and create a competitive market for health care. The single-payer system would abolish all market-place mechanisms because its advocates find virtually all aspects of the marketplace inappropriate to the provision of health services. That argument needs to be answered by the market-driven reform advocates. However, the single-payer reform proposal needs to be evaluated in terms of whether the incentive system and resource allocation mechanism that it would substitute for the marketplace could be as effective as the newly improved, competitive health care market that would be created by a market-driven reform system. Therefore, this chapter will seek to answer, in turn, three questions:

1. Can UHI eliminate the health care market's imperfections?
2. Is a competitive health care market an acceptable or appropriate means for providing health care services?
3. Would a competitive health care system economically outperform a governmental system of providing health care services?

ELIMINATION OF HEALTH CARE MARKET IMPERFECTIONS

The primary way in which market-driven reform seeks to eradicate the existing marketplace imperfections in the health care market is through the restructuring of the health insurance market. When provider cooperatives first developed what came to be known as health insurance in America in the 1920s and '30s, the Blue Cross and Blue Shield plans sold their product as "prepayment," rather than health insurance and they sold prepayment to subscribers, not insureds or customers. It was an outgrowth of the Midwestern cooperative movement of that era. The benefits initially marketed for prepayment were originally all hospital-related services, but did include the surgeon's operating fees, the anesthetist's charge for the anesthesia in surgery, pathology fees for laboratory tests, and the primary care physician's visit while the patient was in the hospital. The term "prepayment" does, indeed, connote the idea that these subscribers in having surgery and staying in the hospital during recuperation have paid in advance for these doctor and hospital services. Naturally, the subscriber would be led to believe that since the services have already been paid for, prices charged would be irrelevant. To further confuse any relationship to a normal buying transaction, those Blue Cross and Blue Shield plans established direct contracts with participating hospitals and doctors (mostly hospital-based physicians) to pay for subscribers' services. When patients checked out of the hospital, they only paid a small amount that had not been prepaid, which in the '60s and '70s frequently came to little more than paying for the use of the television set in the patient's room.

Although the entry of commercial health insurance companies into the health insurance market in the post-World War II era emphasized the insurance aspect of health care prepayment, the Blues' symbolism retained its noninsurance tint, which neither commercial carriers or the subsequent passage of Medicare seriously challenged. Somehow this prepayment-subscriber imagery caught on and stuck, leaving generations of Americans thinking that, at least, hospital-related medical services were different from other services and commodities in the American economy. The same imagery carried over to nonhospital-related physician services and prescription drugs as the health insurance benefit structure was expanded in the '80s and '90s. The noneconomic buying mentality also grew out of the employer-provided health insurance benefit that millions of working Americans came to expect was their due, without realizing that cash wages could have been increased (assuming that employees were given the option and) if employees chose not to be covered by their employers' health insurance benefit. It is no wonder that employees objected so vociferously to the restrictions imposed by managed care plans, which impinged on their employer-provided right to the virtual free use of the American health care system, nor is it difficult to see how hospitals and doctors came to dominate the choice of the type of health care services that Americans were given.

Making Health Insurance into Real Insurance for Consumers
If the federal government were required to provide a comprehensive, first-dollar, health insurance policy to all Americans, who earned incomes below or near (say, 200 percent of) the federal poverty level, the health care market for these Americans would not change appreciably, except that many (approximately 90 percent) of the currently uninsured would be given first-dollar insurance coverage. Indeed, for this income population of our nation, approximately 15 to 20 percent of the total population, there would be no appreciable difference between the health insurance provided by market-driven

99

health insurance reform and the single-payer, governmental model of reform, except that the health care system in which these people would be treated would be vastly different.

The market-driven approach focuses on the middle- and higher-income market—the one in which the buyer can afford to make some purchases of health care without government assistance. The federal government would give every American citizen whose income was substantially above the poverty level a catastrophic health insurance policy promising to pay for all eligible health care services (just to keep it simple) after the family has paid a deductible equal to 10 to 20 percent of that family's income on health care. For the median family income of approximately $45,000, that means a maximum liability of $9,000 a year exists for the 20 percent deductible.

For most median income families who are healthy, the expected level of actual health care expenses is lower than $9,000 unless the families are in the child-bearing age group or have an identified chronic health condition, like diabetes or rheumatoid arthritis. For these families as well as families that are relatively more risk adverse or would prefer a fixed payment schedule over the uncertainty of variations in payments as illnesses or accidents occur, they could buy private health insurance coverage to cover all or part of their deductible, with the knowledge that they could not be denied the right to purchase health insurance because of prior illness. The infamous preexisting conditions clause in health insurance policies will be a thing of the past because health insurers will no longer have any incentive to avoid persons likely to suffer from catastrophic illness, which will be a responsibility of the federal government.

Many healthy American families will choose to be at risk for the full amount of the deductible, as the most economical solution to their health care financing problems, knowing that if a serious illness or accident occurs, they can always borrow the necessary funds through the low-interest federal loan guarantee program—illness never should cause a liquidity problem for American families, nor drive families into bankruptcy as the existing system frequently has done [See Himmelstein et al]. These healthier Americans will receive the maximum increase in wages from their employers' savings in what previously went into employee health insurance benefits.

Regardless of income category, all American families will have to choose a Health Care Financing Agency (HCFA) to serve as their fiscal agent in processing health care bills and to advise them on their health care needs and financing. The role of all HCFAs is to ensure that, once the deductible has been met, all bills for health care become the responsibility of the federal government. Only the HCFA is aware of the family's income—health care providers will be unable to differentiate low income Americans who are entitled to federal benefits from those Americans paying for their own care.

The selection of the most appropriate HCFA for any family will depend on what additional services the family wishes to obtain. If the family wishes to insure itself for some or all of its deductible, then it will probably wish to choose from a number of qualified private health insurance companies that have been certified by the federal government for serving as a HCFA in that geographic area. If, on the other hand, the family has one or more members who are suffering from a chronic illness or illnesses, it may want to both insure for some or all of the deductible and to sign up a more comprehensive health care delivery organization with HCFA status that can provide the specialized patient care services that the family is likely to need. And finally, a healthy family that is unlikely to have many medical needs and wishes to self-insure for the deductible will want to register with a HCFA that can advise families on area health care providers, both medical qualifications and cost reasonableness, so that when medical services are needed the family can wisely choose an appropriate provider. All types of HCFAs are required to have a fully qualified medical advisory service that can advise families about alternative treatment regimes for various illnesses and a 24 hour call-in service for advising with medical emergencies, though the HCFAs could contract this service out to an advisory service that serves multiple HCFAs.

In addition to the changes in the health care consumer's outlook toward the health care market, employed consumers will have a change in their employment relationship. Employees will have to reconsider their employee health insurance benefit because employees will no longer have to insure for the catastrophic coverage and the benefits will no longer be purchased out of tax exempt income. For those employees who wish to continue to purchase health insurance through their employer, the cost of coverage should drop appreciably, by at least a third as we shall explain in the next section. However, employees will have decide whether they want an increase in cash wages, equal to the amount that was the employer's previous cost of health insurance benefits, a smaller wage increase and continue some health insurance coverage for all or some of the costs of the employees' deductible. Many healthy employees will choose the higher wage increase, even though those wages will be subject to income taxes as will any wages spent on health insurance.

The important economic change for fiscally able consumers is that they will be concerned about the prices charged by health care providers. Health care will no longer be a "free service" for most American consumers. The choices they make about the selection of a health care provider or alternative treatment regimes will have economic consequences for most Americans, and hence for doctors and hospitals, or for that matter, pharmacists, drug manufacturers, nursing home operators, etc., etc. Doctors and hospitals will no longer be able to dominate the medical marketplace as they did before the passage of UHI.

Making Health Care Insurable for Insurance Carriers

Similarly, the health insurance market will be revolutionized for health insurance carriers. The 1930s twin concerns of insurance actuaries of adverse selection (selling insurance to persons most likely to be ill enough to utilize their insurance benefits) and the moral hazard of insurance (being insured causes consumers to purchase more health service than they would if they were paying for the services out of their own resources) will be substantially reduced because so many more health care users are, indeed, utilizing their own resources to purchase health care services. Even though persons buying first-dollar comprehensive health insurance will still be subject to some moral hazard of excess health care consumption, there will be a sufficient number of consumers who are totally uninsured in the private market for their deductible to make health care prices reasonably price competitive. More important, private health insurance carriers will now be able to precisely calculate the risks they are accepting when they sell an insurance policy to a family with a particular amount of income because the federal government will be the insurer of last resort for health losses exceeding a fixed amount as determined by the insured's income. A conservative estimate of the savings to private carriers of the federal government's acceptance of the catastrophic insurance function is at least one-third of the premiums currently paid for the entire health insurance package, which is less than the percentage of total health care expenditures made by persons experiencing catastrophic illness. It should be greater than one-third by the time competitive markets have worked their magic in compelling insurers to sharpen their pencils to the nth degree on both the administrative and insurance fees that will have to be paid.

However, private health insurers after the passage of UHI will face a vastly different market in which they too will be subject to the rigors of price competition and the consumer's value-added calculus to survive in the health insurance market. The high administrative cost issue that Himmelstein-Woolhandler has raised about private health insurance is very significant because the consumer and society gets too little value in return for premiums paid for the high prices paid to the current private health insurance function. Currently, private health insurance carriers (including Blue Cross and Blue Shield) are little more than money changers; they serve no risk bearing role and do not provide much information to help consumers make better health care decisions. They will have to do both in the restructured health care system, especially provide useful information to consumers about health care providers' prices, professional credentials, even information on treatment options, and the experiences of various providers with these treatments. The 20 percent profit factor for health insurance carriers will also be a thing of the past, as the health insurance market becomes extremely price competitive. A universal income-related catastrophic health insurance provides an opportunity for existing health insurance companies to survive, but it ensures that they will have to compete to survive. In addition, some private insurers will want to get into the more entrepreneurial role of organizing care for particular disease entities and then serve as the marketing liaison between providers and consumers interested in that kind of care.

The key to making health care into a viable price competitive market is revitalized private health insurance carriers who earn their keep by being true intermediaries between consumers and health care providers. Whether they actually sell insurance to their clients or just serve in the advisory role outlined in the HCFA requirements to families that have chosen to self-insure their deductibles, the private health insurers or their possible successors, like the kind of health care information processing firm Steve Case is trying to initiate (see page 67), will be at the heart of the bargaining-marketing process that will make health care providers respond systematically and economically to consumer demands. Consumers will no longer suffer from a lack of knowledge or understanding of the health care marketplace. Their bargaining will not be done during a medical crisis, but will be in place long before such crises.

Making the Health Care Market Price Competitive

The strategic objective of market-driven health care reform is to create a price competitive marketplace that will be the equal of other private markets in the American economy and, thus, to end hospital-physician dominance both in terms of prices and in the selection of the style of medicine practiced in the United States. The federal government can, through the passage of income-related catastrophic health insurance coverage for all Americans, serve to bring the health care market into conformance with the rest of the economy. From the Chapter 2 discussion of the imperfect health care market, the estimated savings of bringing effective price competition to the health care market are in the order of 20 to 25 percent of personal health care expenditures, more than the savings single-payer advocates believe could be saved in eliminating the administrative costs through a government operated health care system. The difference in approach is what one set of reformers see as a waste, the market-driven see as opportunity to bring increased value to the health care system by changing the insurer's role into coordinator, bargainer, and information disseminator to help the American consumer in making effective and efficient health care decisions. By having health care providers charge the same price to each of its purchasers, administrative costs for providers will be drastically reduced. In addition, competitive pressures should sharply reduce profitability margins of health insurance companies. A restructured health marketplace is capable of providing all the advantages that Americans take for granted in the rest of their private market economy. It's the innovative response of different competitors in private markets that has led to the improved welfare of industrialized nations through increased productivity and economic growth that has reduced the number of people living in poverty [Rosenberg and Birdzell].

In the American economy, the competitive market's primary compulsion is to make producers search for innovative, lower cost ways to produce products and/or to design new and better products and services while consumers are free to choose which and how many of these products and services they wish to purchase—the market's test of success. In the health care marketplace, price competition will change the incentives from meeting provider demands to satisfying consumer values—higher quality, safer, and less costly services. For example, the nation's best health care system, the VA's, is providing very high quality, safe, and less costly care for America's veterans through the use of a computerized medical record and patient identification system that requires physicians and nurses to record all patient information into a wireless laptop computer. Even though the VA has made its system software freely available to the private sector, no private health care organization has downloaded and employed the system because private sector physicians have refused to be tethered to laptop computers [Longman]. In the current provider-dominated health care system it is their values that control the system, not consumer values. Bringing competitive markets to health care will return control of the American health care system to consumers. Physicians will learn to love the computer, or suffer the loss of patient care revenues to other organizations that do enhance consumer values. Indeed, if there is excess capacity in the VA system, it would be useful and educational to allow the VA to compete with private health delivery organizations in those excess-capacity markets.

No one or no group can control a free market; the market system is an independent process—similar to Darwin's view of nature—that operates continuously as competing producers interact with consumers. It is the lack of control that drives some people's concerns about free market capitalism, especially among fundamentalists or absolutists who "know" what the outcome must be. In a price competitive free market, the behavior of capitalists (multi-national or otherwise and regardless of size) is constrained by the presence of competitors to pay fair wages and follow societal environmental standards. The fact that no one is in charge of a free market can be liberating and ensuring to the many as well as threatening to special interests previously in control, as physicians and hospitals have been in the health care market.

Impediments to Free Competive Markets

On the other hand, businesses, through monopolization and price fixing, can reduce market effectiveness by siphoning off benefits in illegitimate profits and slowing down the rate of innovation. In this case, government has an obligation to intervene to stop such anti-competitive practices. Businesses, like everyone, do not enjoy being compelled to be efficient and to be always searching for new and better ways to produce new and better products. The competitive process is relentless and so exhausting that it creates a counter incentive to escape the market compulsion to always be changing and improving. Mancur Olson [151-52], who taught economics at the University of Maryland and had specialized in collusive market behavior, observed that stable economic and political environments are more likely to allow the development of barriers to innovation and change than more dynamic political economies. The desire to create barriers may even be stronger during periods of volatility, but firms are less able to build impediments to competition, as the health care market should be immediately after passage of UHI, than during more stable periods.

Businesses would be relieved to be able to rest on their laurels, at least periodically. The temptation is great. Because the market compulsion is uniform among competitors, perhaps the easiest means of gaining a respite from the never-ending pressure of market competition is collusion. Especially in industries with a small number of large firms, it may be possible to conspire with competitors to fix prices or to agree not to compete in certain product or geographic markets. The private health insurance market is taking on this type of market structure [Robinson] and should be monitored to ensure that collusion does not occur during the implementation of the UHI program. Even though the average firm's profits are slightly less than what the successful competitor might have earned, who knows which particular firms would have been the winners in a truly competitive market? Total profits of all the conspiring firms may not even be that much higher than the firms would have earned in a competitive market, at least immediately after the conspiracy was hatched. What would be lost, however, is the incentive for each of the firms to innovate, to find new and better ways to produce new and better products. The implementation of the new UHI program will mark a significant opportunity for great innovation in health care delivery. Thus, it is important for governments to enact and to enforce legislation discouraging anticompetitive behavior or the monopolization of commerce, collectively described under antitrust laws.

Fortunately, these kinds of conspiracies or cartels, lacking a central authority, are often very unstable and difficult to maintain voluntarily. The temptation for firms to cheat their co-conspirators is great. In addition to cheating conspirators, the market itself generally has the means to break up market collusion through the entry of new competitors who are attracted to the market by the higher than normal profits being earned by the conspirators. Both Schumpeter [1942] and Olson [59] believed that free entry into markets is a "staggeringly powerful" antidote to anti-competitive behavior. And further, if the participants are competing in global markets under conditions of free trade in either the factors (capital and labor) employed in producing the goods and services or the final goods and services themselves, collusive behavior is extremely difficult, if not impossible, to achieve [Olson, 142]. Even the health care industry is becoming increasingly global as more Americans travel to Asia for surgical procedures at a fraction of American costs.

However, the most insidious form of collusion to overcome the power of competitive markets involves the use of government authority. Market participants conspire with elements of the political system through special interest legislation or special regulatory rulings to strengthen the competitive position of particular businesses. Tax-supported subsidies are given to products; e.g., subsidies for agricultural products in the United States and in many other developed nations are the most egregious example of this form of business-government "conspiracies." Agricultural price subsidies are legislated so openly in response to the political pressures of the so-called farm-bloc that it is hard to think of this practice as conspiratorial, but since there is no prohibition against special interest legislation, there is no need to be secretive. And finally, favorable treatment in market regulation of certain industries is the third form of business-induced collusion with government; the congressional involvement in the Food and Drug Administration's regulation of the pharmaceutical industry is probably the most troublesome domestic illustration, but Congress has a broad field of opportunity in providing "constituency" support.

Aside from the pharmaceutical industry concern and the need to carefully observe the behavior of health insurance carriers during the early years of UHI implementation, the health care market should be able to adapt to the new price competition resulting from the restructuring of health insurance with the innovative spirit that has marked the rest of the U.S. economy. Health care in the United States should become relatively less expensive, much more innovative, as well as more equitably distributed through the passage of UHI.

MORAL ACCEPTABILITY OF MARKETS FOR HEALTH CARE

Even if significant enhancement of the health care industry's economic performance could be achieved through UHI, Himmelstein and Woolhandler (H-W) remain suspicious of market mechanisms for the delivery of health care services. H-W are concerned that the profit motive is morally inconsistent with the humanitarian objective of patient care. Such criticism of free markets is not unusual. Some religions and other social critics go beyond honest differences in defining equity to wholly reject free market economies as fundamentally immoral because, they argue, the spirit of acquisitiveness or "greed" underlies the basic motives for the marketplace to operate effectively. H-W certainly fit into this group of market critics, at least as applied to health care. Advocates of the free market do not see market competition as immoral but rather as amoral, not imposing any moral judgments on market participants. Conduct in markets, however, reflects societal moral values and is regulated by a nation's laws, such as laws prohibiting slavery or the sale of human organs, and individual behavior is subject to a person's moral precepts, whether it be honoring the Sabbath or abstaining from the use of debt capital. The amorality of markets does not imply that markets sanction immoral behavior. Markets don't sanction anything; only governments can sanction behavior. Market operations reflect the general beliefs and mores of the society in which individuals are pursuing their interests in a manner consistent with their personal morals and society's laws. Regardless of who agrees, the market's operation reflects consumer values, rather than determining them authoritatively.

The Role of Profits

Profits are crucial in the allocation of resources, especially capital, among alternative uses, which is the definition of economic science—the study of the allocation of scarce resources among alternative and competing uses. Profits provide both incentives for investors to commit resources to particular uses and information upon which to invest. When returns from one particular area of investment start to decline, investors search for other alternatives that are producing higher rates of return. One of the peculiar difficulties of the H-W proposal for a governmental health care system is that their profitless approach has no similar objective criteria for making the resource allocation decisions in their health care system. The single-payer approach outlaws the use of for-profit organizations in the provision of health care services after a fifteen year transition period, and, as we have seen, only vaguely suggests a regional-state planning mechanism for allocating capital among competing investment projects. However, that particular problem will be discussed in the next major section that evaluates the economic performances of the two reform prototypes.

The market-driven reformers must first address the issue of excess profits being charged by greedy capitalists. A recent article in the *New York Times* about Genentech, one of the most successful new genetic drug manufacturers, illustrates the tough issue of what can be done currently about pharmaceutical manufacturers that charge exorbitant prices for a new wonder drug for cancer treatment whose co-payments alone will price the drug out of the range for most persons with prescription drug insurance, to say nothing about persons without insurance. The drug is Avastin, a drug that has been widely prescribed for colon cancer at a cost of approximately $50,000 a year, but is now considered medically effective for breast and lung cancer. If Genentech maintained the same unit price, the increased dosage and longer period of treatment translates into a charge of $100,000 a year per patient for treating these additional disease entities, according to a newly formulated pricing theory that Genentech's president, Dr. Susan Desmon-Hellmann, has described as being based on "the value of innovation, and the value of new therapies," [Berenson] which seem to imply that the value of innovation means a pharmaceutical monopolist can charge "whatever the market will bear." Advancing this concept of pricing generated a host of opposing letters to the editor of the Times and critical comments on web sites.

Pharmaceutical pricing of drugs has always been subject to considerable controversy due to the manufacturers' argument that the development of new drugs requires very expensive research and development costs that must be recovered in the prices of these new drugs. It is to recover these R & D costs that drug manufacturing companies are granted patent protection for 20 years from filing for newly developed drugs—the period in which the manufacturer can recover these costs. Critics of the pharmaceutical industry argue that the cost of advertising and promotion of new drugs often cost more than the original development. The patent laws have also been subject to a great deal of manipulation by drug manufacturers by bringing out new "improved" versions of the original patented drug as a technique for extending the protection time for another 20 years when, in fact, the changes are extremely minute and simply a dodge to extend the patent protection. Drug prices drop significantly when the patent expires and other manufacturers can market generic versions of the previously patent-restricted drugs. However, foreign governments with national health insurance programs have employed monopsony purchasing practices that have driven down the prices they are willing to pay for American drugs—a practice that the single-payer advocates plan to duplicate. Thus, the American market is virtually the only one in which the full amortization of R & D costs has been allowed, resulting in Americans paying higher prices for drugs than consumers in most foreign countries. Pricing under this more amorphous concept of innovative value would almost certainly lead to calls for Congress to initiate federal price regulation of the pharmaceutical industry—something that the single-payer reform approach also plans to undertake.

Drug pricing has always been a quandary for economists and public policy analysts, for there is more than a modicum of truth to the pharmaceutical manufacturers' argument that profits are needed to get firms to invest in the research necessary to discover new drugs, but how much profit is needed? There are few objective tests that may be used to answer that question. One can take a rather arbitrary action and allow the single-payer reformers' regulators to cut profits until research ceases and than raise profits slightly and hope that the new research will be effective. That seems, however, to be a rather dangerous way to make public policy when the stakes for the future of humankind in terms of longevity and quality of life could be very high.

Drug pricing raises other public policy issues. Under either health insurance reform proposal, high drug prices would not prevent Americans from receiving particular drugs as long as physicians concur that use is medically necessary and is likely to provide benefit from the drugs. It should be noted, however, that in the market-driven approach those who could afford to pay for a portion or all of the drug costs would be required to do so. In the case of Avastin, the likely benefit for colon-cancer patients is an average of about five months of extended life at a cost nearly $10,000 for each month of additional life. How much cost can our society afford to pay for each month of extended living? What is the value of a month of life? One might use data from the experience of the wealthy to see how much those who could afford to pay out of their own pockets are willing to pay—certainly society shouldn't be willing to pay more. Many patients that can afford Avastin, depending on their age, health, and family relationships, simply refuse to spend that much out of their own pockets for that kind of life extension. A cure for their disease would undoubtedly be judged to be much more valuable and command a much higher acceptable price.

Part of the reason for the success of the free market approach is that markets rationally decide how much profit is enough for investors and how much people are willing to pay for various levels of benefits. These sorts of questions are very difficult for government to answer as rationally. However, both sets of reform advocates need to recognize that establishing limits on how much government should spend on various components of national or universal health insurance benefits will have to be answered. The single-payer advocates will have many more questions to answer than the market-driven advocates who will, whenever possible, depend on market solutions to indicate the balance between cost and benefit, but some questions, like the amount that society can afford to pay for each month of extended life, will require more arbitrary answers that only governments are entitled to give.

On the other hand, there may also be a problem when a particular drug, which has great benefit to society like certain vaccines, but drug manufacturers find the costs, including future liabilities for adverse drug reactions, too high to justify production. In this case, the federal government has had to step in to either subsidize manufacturing costs or limit producer liability as it as done with certain flu vaccines. Market reform through UHI would not end the need for this sort of government intervention into the marketplace.

Potential Harm to Patients

The reason for H-W rejection of for-profit health care delivery organizations is their concern that the pursuit of profits may lead to the increased risk of injury to patients from medically unneeded or even dangerous services. However, the H-W plan does accept the fee-for-service payment mechanism for the provision of health services and that payment mechanism has exactly the same incentives for over-utilization of services that a profit incentive does. The allegation that doctors practicing fee-for-service medicine put their patients into risk situations by over-prescribing services to earn higher incomes is frequently made and the Professional Standards Review Organizations were federally established in the 1970s to safeguard against over-utilization of services. Interestingly, both H-W and the American Medical Association would give the same one-word defense against the overutilization, "professionalism;" physicians take the Hippocratic Oath to do no harm to their patients. In addition, professional associations and state licensing bodies have review mechanisms and disciplinary boards to censure doctors that fail to meet professional standards of patient care. When all else fails, free market advocates believe that physicians injuring patients should be held liable for malfeasance or malpractice in state and federal courts just like any other producer of goods or services, even though existing malpractice laws may require reform. These precautions or disincentives to prevent abuses of physician privilege are adequate safeguards to protect patients from both the occasional bad doctor and for-profit organizations providing substandard services to patients. The H-W prohibition against profit-making in health care is unnecessarily redundant and removes the profit incentive as a device for allocating resources in the American health care delivery system.

ECONOMIC SUPERIORITY OF MARKETS

Evidence of the superiority of markets in providing information and incentives to allocate resources maximally for societies is abundant, but does that proven superiority of markets over government mechanisms of resource allocation hold true for the health care market? The issue that market-driven reform advocates must explain to obtain support for their reform proposal is the validity of the claim that the efficiency of markets can be brought to the medical marketplace. We have posited that the fundamental problem in the health care market is structural and that restructuring the health insurance component can result in the advantages that other markets possess. There are, however, other problems that economists have noted about the medical marketplace. In the first subsection of market effectiveness discussion, those other shortcomings about the medical marketplace will be considered. We will, then, compare the kinds of resource allocation and consumer incentive issues that the single-payer advocates must overcome before rejecting the UHI solution of America's health care system problems. And finally, we conclude the section and the chapter with a summary of the economic advantages markets have over a governmentally operated health care system.

Other Shortcomings of Medical Marketplace

Health economists have been trying to explain and to recommend policies for fixing the problems in the health market since the subspecialty emerged from the general economics discipline in the mid-1960s. From the outset the approach of health economists has been to emphasize the ways in which the health care market differs from the markets for other goods and services. And it is very different, but these initial doubts about whether health care markets could efficiently allocate and consume resources very much colored the development of this new economics subspecialty. In the early 1960s the Ford Foundation, as part of its campaign to generate interest in the study of health economics, commissioned a study of the health care market by

Kenneth J. Arrow [1963], a preeminent Stanford economist and subsequently a Nobel laureate in economics, to do "an exploratory and tentative study of the specific differentia of medical care as the object of normative economics."

Arrow's study has proven to be anything but tentative. It presented a catalogue of imperfections in the health care market that concluded "the special structural characteristics of the medical-care market are largely attempts to overcome the lack of optimality due to the nonmarketability of the bearing of suitable risks and the imperfect marketability of information."

He saw little opportunity for making the health market efficient and defended the "use of other social institutions...[to] step into the optimality gap...to achieve optimality by nonmarket means." In addition to the need for government to assume public health and income redistribution responsibilities, Arrow focused on flaws in the private health insurance market, on the knowledge disparity between physician and patient, and on the need for patients' trust in their physicians.

The litany of differences and special circumstances is long, but Arrow did not cite the difference in knowledge between the insurer and the insured. The relationship between patients and physicians is still very special and personal. Because of the differences in knowledge, trust between buyer (patients) and seller (physicians) is a more important part of the doctor-patient relationship than in the buying and selling of many other services. In addition, society allowed the use of price discrimination (different prices to buyers for the same service) so that physicians could finance free or low cost care to the financially disadvantaged by charging higher prices to the affluent. Many of the other organizations involved in delivery (e.g., the vast majority of hospitals) and financing (all the Blue Cross and Shield plans) of health care were not-for-profit, and thus, less commercial (and competitive) than for-profit businesses. These nonprofit entities also practiced society-sanctioned price discrimination. And finally, insuring health care is quite different from insuring other losses, principally because the insured has greater control of covered losses than is the case with other forms of casualty losses, such as theft or fire insurance where a loss is dependent on the action of an independent party or event.

Employer-sponsored private health insurance became the biggest anomaly of all. Employees preferred to take a portion of their wages in the form of health insurance benefits instead of cash, take-home pay, especially when the federal government chose not to tax these benefits as income. And employers for several decades did not mind dodging the tax collector by offering a larger portion of salaries in bigger and better health benefits. First or low-dollar coverage of comprehensive hospital-related health services, with freedom to choose any provider, became the norm for employment-based health insurance. Later, this model of health insurance became the prototype for fashioning Medicare and Medicaid in the 1960s at about the time the subspecialty of health economics was emerging.

During its first two decades of development the mainstream of health economics accepted these market idiosyncrasies as necessary for overcoming fundamental problems of buying and selling health care and health insurance without the normal skepticism that marks the study of economics and the mindset of economists. Most important, the institutional arrangements for financing health insurance through employment, which became so very popular during and after World War II by holding out the promise of "free" health care, should long ago have instinctively raised the hackles of a profession dedicated to the proposition that "there is no free lunch." Alas, it did not, and the consequences were serious to the development of health economics. Many health economists, accepting Arrow's assessment, have simply given up on the competitive market solution for the health care marketplace.

In light of this skepticism by so many health economists, we will systematically examine each of the cited market shortcomings in the health economics literature and review how the income-related catastrophic health insurance proposal meets the economists' concerns. The first and perhaps strongest indictment of conditions in the medical marketplace was Arrow's concern was "the nonmarketability of bearing suitable risks and the imperfect marketability of information." The need for the federal government to assume the role of insurer of last resort has been recommended specifically because the problem of the private insurance market's inability to deal with adverse risk selection, and, as reported earlier in the chapter, to reduce the risks that are insured in the private insurance markets to actuarially insurable risks. The federal government is the appropriate agency in the economy to bear the ultimate risks of ill-health for all of society. In a sense, the need for government intervention in the health insurance market is consistent with Arrow's analysis. Nothing could be a more appropriate role for government than to remove this uninsurable risk from the private health insurance market.

Even though Arrow did not address the insurer's imperfect knowledge about the health of the person being insured, which would be made irrelevant by the federal government's assumption of the catastrophic health risks, he did emphasize that a difference frequently cited in the economics literature is the disparity in knowledge (or information) between the patient and the treating physician, which it is argued makes it much more difficult for the patient to make informed decisions. Again, the income-related catastrophic health insurance proposal has tried to address this problem by creating a new market for the creation and sale of independent medical information through the requirement that the HCFA must provide this information service to all persons who register with the HCFA. Whether this function enhances or detracts from the personal relationship between the physician and patient depends on the soundness of the advice provided by the physician to the patient. If the physician's advice is sound and is, therefore, confirmed by the independent advisor, that relationship should be strengthened. On the other hand, if a physician's advice is frequently challenged by the independent advisor, the consumer may well develop questions about the competence of his/her physician, as should be the case. The overall effect of the installing an independent source of medical information should be a relationship of greater equality between patient and physician. How some physicians will deal with such a new state affairs should be interesting to observe.

All of the other abnormalities in the health care market that come from the different way in which health insurance was sold, the involvement of not-for-profit organizations in the health insurance and health care delivery markets, the gross inequities that arose in the employment basis, and the overabundance of first-dollar private health insurance coverage should be eradicated by the UHI program. Income-related catastrophic health insurance for those financially able to pay a portion of their health care costs and a medical care advisor for all consumers should make the health care market perform like the competitive markets in the rest of the U.S. economy. The health care industry should become equally innovative and lower cost as a result of this program, as well as making health more equitably available to all Americans. It will also be extremely interesting to observe how some of the more overly confident or even arrogant physicians will handle a more egalitarian relationship with their patients.

Resource Allocation in Single-Payer System

In contrast to the more efficiently functioning health care system, the single-payer, governmentally operated health care system will have two specific problems: (1) by eliminating patient responsibility for copayments and deductibles the NHI proposal makes health care a free good; and (2) by eliminating all profits in the health care system, except pharmaceutical products that are price-controlled, government bureaucracies will have to perform all of the allocations of capital among alternative uses in the health care industry. Both problems will inevitably lead to rationing health care services among the citizenry and capital among health facilities and the necessary politicization of a whole host of resource allocation decisions to a much greater and more widespread degree than in the UHI approach. Both reform systems will, however, require at least some rationing of health services.

A zero price for health services for all consumers in the single-payer approach will quickly exhaust all of the administrative savings that the elimination of private health insurance carriers generated. Indeed, according to the estimates of the Rand Health Insurance Experiment, a 50 percent increase in the consumption of health services can be expected for those consumers who had been paying a substantial amount of copayments or deductibles prior to the inception of NHI. A rough and probably low estimate of the number of Americans who will receive a substantial reduction in the price of health care services is 66 million people—42 million uninsured, 10 million Medicare beneficiaries without supplemental coverage, and 14 million persons covered by nongroup private health insurance. That is quite a substantial increase in the demand for health care services if nearly a quarter of all Americans suddenly got free health services. In addition all other Americans will receive lesser but nevertheless some reductions in the price of health care services.

In all likelihood, the health care system's capacity to deliver such a large increase in services at the outset of the new program will immediately lead to queuing of patients; i.e., waiting lines for appointments with physicians or to schedule procedures. The dilemma for the health care system will be sorting out differences in the urgency of patients needs to see that the sicker, more urgent patients receive prompter care. In hospital emergency rooms, this process of sorting out patients in terms of the urgency of the need for patient care is done by the triage nurse who interviews patients to make a quick diagnosis of the medical problem and assign an urgency index to the patients; e.g., patients with sore throats and diarrhea are seen after patients with broken limbs or patients experiencing chest pains, for example. The way other countries, like Great Britain or Canada, with national health insurance programs have done the triaging is by assigning lower urgency ratings to whole classes of health care problems; e.g., elective surgery is usually given a low rating and fewer resources are assigned to this function, which is a way of allocating resources to a more urgent medical need, but it does cause long waits of many months or even years to patients needing various kinds of elective surgeries, like hernia repairs and hip or knee replacements. This is what may be appropriately called macro-rationing because preferences are established for the whole system to accomplish the rationing function.

American support of equality usually doesn't include much patience for long waiting lines; Americans are always trying to expedite matters by finding a way to get to the head of those lines, frequently with wealthier Americans buying their way to the front of the line. Indeed, even the British and Canadians who do include more patience in their approach to equalitarianism have found it necessary to relieve queuing pressures by allowing citizens to opt out of the governmental health care system into a private health care system. The British have tolerated the private alternative for a long time. However, the Canadian national health care system, interestingly called Medicare, has prohibited any opt out in the country. They couldn't stop Canadians from leaving the country to obtain health care in the United States, but the Canadian law prohibited the private sale of health care services in the country until quite recently. However, last June (2005) the Supreme Court in Canada:

> ruled that long waits for various medical procedures in the province
> [of Quebec] had violated patients' 'life and personal security,
> inviolability' and that the prohibition of private health insurance
> was unconstitutional when the public health system did not deliver
> 'reasonable services.' [Quebec has subsequently proposed to] lift a
> ban on private health insurance for selective surgical procedures
> and announced that it would pay for such surgeries at private clinics
> when the waiting times at public facilities was unreasonable
> [Krauss].

Nevertheless, the Canadian government will not permit medical personnel to work both in public and private facilities as the British do. All Canadian physicians must choose the type of facility—public or private—in which they wish to practice, although the more conservative province of Alberta has proposed to permit physicians to work simultaneously in both types of facilities and would allow patients to pay cash for services in private facilities [Cherney].

The remarkable fact in the Canadian case is that it took so long (more than 45 years) for the queuing phenomenon to bubble to the surface and cause this political and legal dispute. We can safely predict that Americans would not wait nearly as long to challenge the prohibition on private payment for health care services in the United States as HR676 proposes. Indeed, if Americans were forced to wait for medical services as long as British and Canadian have had to wait, we might have the Second American Revolution, this time against the British/Canadian medical system as practiced in America with its macro-rationing.

The other form of rationing is what might be called micro-rationing that occurs in defining allowable care for specific individuals and their illnesses. It stems from very high cost therapies, especially for terminally-ill patients, which have a low probability of curing the patient but could result in extending life. It's very similar to the Avastin case discussed on pages 110 and 112 in which a cancer patient is able to obtain additional months of life. In these sorts of cases in which the benefit is difficult to quantify but costs can be extremely high, the health care system under the single-payer, governmental approach would be forced to establish arbitrary bureaucratic rules and budgetary limits on providing treatment. Perhaps in some parts of the country where health care organizations have budgetary surpluses, the treatment will be approved, but in other areas with less generous budgetary allotments, the treatment will be denied.

Micro-rationing in the single-payer system really raises a more fundamental resource allocation problem: How are funds allocated to various organizations and regions around the country? Most likely, at the outset of the program, resources will be allocated according to what is being spent in an area or by an organization in the year prior to the inauguration of the program. Developing criteria and rules for changing the original allocation decisions is extremely difficult without markets. Further, the general incentive for any organization functioning under a governmental budgetary system is to spend the annual budget, otherwise next year's allocation will be smaller. It certainly doesn't provide any real incentive to economize and look for different ways to improve the way services are delivered. That is the age old problem with governments that will be discussed in the first section of the next chapter, which contrasts the role of government to stabilize and defend the status quo with the role of markets as a mechanism to innovate and to change.

As was noted in the original discussion of the Avastin case, the income-related catastrophic program also has a problem with the micro-rationing problem that exists in that program for first-dollar insurance beneficiaries and persons who have met their deductible limit and are now fully qualified for federal catastrophic coverage. For these beneficiaries, there is no longer any price constraint affecting their consumption decisions. Although that could lead to the same problem that occurs for all consumers in the single-payer approach, the designers of the market-driven approach have tried to incorporate some features into the income-related catastrophic program to act as safeguards for making rational resource allocation decisions. First, for low income beneficiaries with chronic conditions, such diabetes, rheumatoid arthritis, or lung or coronary diseases, these patients would be required to enroll with a HCFA-HMO in their area that specializes or has expertise in treating their particular illness. The idea is to create market competition in the supplier market for treatment of these illnesses as a means of economizing in the cost of caring for these very high cost consumers. For higher income catastrophically ill persons, the program requires experimental state programs to be developed by state government agencies that will search for similar kinds of program for treating patients with these particular diseases. The problem for market reformers is that the market, at least on the demand side, cannot work for consumers that are not bound by a price constraint, so imaginative mechanisms must created to alter the way in medical services are provided.

Reform That Is Economically Superior

The problem just described of micro-rationing can best be solved with lots of experimentation at the state level and not through arbitrary bureaucratic rules and allocations, as the single-payer approach would require for all consumers and in developing health care organizations throughout the country. Indeed, in general markets are economically superior to government allocation systems. It was for that reason that capitalism triumphed economically over communism in the Cold War, even though some communist economic theorists tried to create systems of transfer pricing that could replicate markets. Their efforts failed and so would a single-payer, governmentally operating NHI program. Government planning is no match for a reformed health care market in terms of efficiency.

The Rand Health Insurance Experiment found that health care costs were nearly one-third less for persons with relatively large deductibles, or at least 25 percent coinsurance provisions, than for individuals having free care (first-dollar coverage) like the single-pay approach [Newhouse 1993]. Furthermore, there was no observable effect on health except for lower-income families. Specifically, Newhouse [1993, 344] "observed certain adverse health consequences in the Experiment from cost sharing, concentrated among the sick poor." The effect of cost sharing on the poor is the reason income-related catastrophic plan includes no deductibles or copayments for those below 200 percent of the poverty line. In addition to greater savings than would occur through the administrative cost reductions that the single-payer NHI program would realize, the system of health care in United States would take on an innovative style that is likely to produce even greater cost savings in revitalized health care delivery organizations that must compete for consumers on the basis of the prices they charge. The reformed health care industry will finally takes its place along side other American enterprises that have achieved worldwide economic superiority.

BIBLIOGRAPHY

Arrow, K., "Uncertainty and the Welfare Economics of Medical Care," *American Economic Review*, Vol. 53, No. 4 (December 1963), pp. 941-973.

Berenson, A., "A Cancer Drug Shows Promise, at a Price That Many Can't Pay," *New York Times*, February 15, 2006.

Cherney, E., "Canada Relents on Health Care," *Wall Street Journal*, March 7, 2006.

Himmelstein, D.U., Warren, E., Thorne, D., and Woolhandler, S., "Illness and Injury as Contributors to Bankruptcy," *Health Affairs Web Exclusive*, W5-63, February 2, 2005.

Krauss, C., "Ruling Has Canada Planting Seeds of Private Health Care," *New York Times*, Feb-ruary 20, 2006.

Longman, P., "The Best Care Anywhere," *Washington Monthly*, January/February 2005, http://www.washingtonmonthly.com/features/2005/0501.longman.html.

Newhouse, J.P., and the Insurance Experiment Group, *Free for All? Lessons from the Rand Health Insurance Experience Group*, Cambridge, MA: Harvard University Press, 1993.

Olson, M., *The Rise and Decline of Nations: Economic Growth, Stagflation, and Social Rigidities*, New Haven: Yale University Press, 1982.

Robinson, J.C., "Consolidation and the Transformation of Competition in Health Insurance," *Health Affairs*, Vol. 23, No.6 (November/December 2004), pp. 11-24.

Rosenberg, N., and Birdzell, L.E., Jr. *How the West Grew Rich: The Economic Transformation of the Industrial* World, New York: Basic Books, Inc., 1986.

Schumpeter, J.A. *Capitalism, Socialism, and Democracy*, 6th ed. London: Unwin Paperbacks, 1987, first edition 1942.

CHAPTER 4
The Politics of Enacting
Either NHI or UHI

As the Chapter 1 historical analysis of past health reform legislation (pages 25 to 32) suggested, getting Congress and the President to agree on a bipartisan national or universal health insurance proposal will be extremely difficult. Repeated efforts have been made over the 90 years since 1916 when a committee of Congress was first appointed to study the issue and the search began to reach an agreement on federal health insurance among the two legislative bodies and America's chief elected official. Universal health insurance, as a separate concept wasn't even conceived until the 1970s when both Presidents Nixon and Ford introduced legislation that would have mandated the purchase of health insurance by employers. Both NHI and UHI plans raise strong ideological issues with our elected federal officials. We begin by first describing the nature of government, then discussing those ideological issues that stand between liberals and conservatives in the debate over health insurance, and finally move on to discuss the practical politics of the winners and losers in the health care and related industries and different voting blocks. The chapter concludes by discussing the conclusion that a UHI proposal would serve as a better possible compromise.

THE NATURE OF GOVERNMENT

The source of difficulty in passing grand reforms like health insurance is at the heart of the advantage of employing markets rather than depending on government actions to maintain a dynamic, growing society. Markets are simply an organized mechanism for buyers and sellers (people) to conduct transactions, but this mechanism forces changes autonomously whenever someone in the marketplace has a better idea for a new product or process for making existing products. Because the change agents, entrepreneurs, risk their own capital in implementing ideas, markets provide an autonomous and rapid systematic feedback on the merit of ideas, which serve as a self-correcting or tuning mechanism for modifying ideas that aren't quite right. In a competitive marketplace without barriers to entry, the implementation of a good or better idea is extremely difficult to prevent.

Conversely, government actions are resistant to change. Self-interest works as an accelerator for change in markets by motivating market players to find new and better ideas and works like brakes on change in the governmental or political arena where people and groups who have advantage try to preserve those advantages and where bureaucrats are not paid to take risks and, indeed, many may have entered public service to avoid personal risk-taking. Moreover, unlike an open market, government programs are frequently protected by restrictions on new competition, or government have occasionally granted monopoly powers to a favored individual, firm, or industry.

Government must provide a safeguard for existing institutions, which has some beneficial results. Even the most law-abiding citizens would find it difficult to avoid crime if the legal code were continually changing. The law, as a framework for individual action, must be consistent and stable. While markets change automatically and incrementally in response to altered tastes, resource supplies, or technology, government policies typically change only in large, discrete steps, often with a long lag after the initial stimulus for change. Markets allow variation in individual response—we can buy a product or ignore it. Government programs tend to enforce conformity. Finally, while government ultimately must recognize costs and benefits, it allows program beneficiaries to ignore them in specific programs. Market activity forces participants to weight costs against benefits—we seek to get what we pay for. Since costs measure the value of alternatives foregone, decisions made in the market foster efficient use of resources. Activity through government offers citizens or groups to shift the costs of their actions to others—competitors, consumers, or taxpayers. In short, rent-seeking is possible through using government to shift the cost of one's action onto others. And where individuals can focus exclusively on programs' costs or benefits to them, they are likely to foster inefficiency. The infamous earmarks that individual Congressmen can attach to budget appropriations without control is a perfect example of rent seeking—a government program that benefits only a small group of voters at a relatively small cost to others, but whose aggregate effect with many Congressmen taking advantage of the slipshod rules can become a significant problem in containing the total costs of government operations.

Consequently, significant modifications, let alone reversals, of programs generated by political action are very difficult to enact. Almost all major political reforms require a very unique set of circumstances for passage, like, for instance, Medicare in 1965 when the aged were priced out of the private health insurance market by experience rating. Programs' advantages must be overwhelming, or costs trivial (as in the requirement that everyone drive on the right side of the road), if easy passage is to be obtained. In cases involving substantial cost as well as benefits, achieving political consensus is usually difficult. Since government programs affect all citizens whether they favor the programs or not, both support and opposition are highly probable.

Virtually all existing legislation benefits some group, either directly or through opportunities to administer it. At the same time, there will always be those who feel harmed by the same laws. The forces of the status quo often are especially motivated to oppose change; they know the benefits they obtain, and these benefits are often concentrated on a small minority of citizens. Proponents of change, however, must sell the promise of improvement. Often the gains from improvement, while large in aggregate, are widely dispersed. Under such conditions, small but passionate minorities may exert more influence than larger but less motivated majorities. Making reforms or changes through the political process requires overcoming the resistance to change of those whose best interest is served by maintaining the status quo, and the loudest feedback politicians proposing reforms receive is the squeals of objections from the parties whose interests are being threatened by the idea.

Consider the difficulty of closing military posts, for example. Political proponents are often dispersed and find it harder to organize, even when they have more to gain than status quo advocates who believe they will lose by the passage of reform legislation. Both structurally and temperamentally, the U.S. political system is as protective of the status quo as its markets are committed to continuous change. In politics, the opportunity for self-interested parties to prevent changes from being undertaken is substantially greater than, at least, legally-sanctioned blocking tactics in the marketplace.

Markets have one other advantage over politics. When a political change is accepted, there is no automatic feedback device for correcting inferior change ideas, which requires admitting mistakes. In fact, the difficulty of correcting an imperfect reform may be almost as great as originally enacting those reforms, which may explain why American politicians are so cautious about change, especially in programs they have helped to enact. Given sufficient time imperfect ideas can also develop their own protective, self-interest constituencies who will work to stifle further legislative change that might diminish their advantage.

Labor laws are an excellent example of the difficulty of enacting the initial reform and its subsequent modification. Since the latter part of the 19th century, labor unions, primarily through the courts, had fought, with limited success, for organizing and negotiating rights to represent employees in collective bargaining agreements. The time for their reform finally came in the Great Depression when a Democratic president, Franklin Roosevelt, and a Democratically-controlled

Congress enacted the Wagner-Connery Act of 1935, which established a National Labor Relations Board (NLRB) to protect the rights of employees to organize and choose representatives for collective bargaining with businesses engaged in interstate commerce. Management subsequently argued that the pendulum of reform had swung too far in labor's favor, especially during the postwar labor strife. But it was able only in the brief window of opportunity in the 80th Congress (1947-48) to replace the Wagner-Connery Act with the Taft-Hartley Act of 1948 over President Truman's veto. This reform of the initial labor-collective bargaining reform kept NLRB machinery but redefined "unfair bargaining" tactics and added injunctive relief for strikes affecting the national interest and a cooling-off period before strikes to strengthen bargaining. With only minor periodic tinkering, that law provided the basic framework for labor-management relationships ever since.

Properly functioning markets are vastly better change mechanisms than the most democratically-organized governments. Nevertheless, governments have a vital role in making markets work properly and one for which stability is beneficial. Governments must guarantee adherence to the rule of law that protects property and contract rights to enable commerce, enact rules to ensure market fairness, including labor, antitrust, and financial reporting laws, and judicially enforce competitive market conduct. Only if governments carry out this role effectively can societies that want to have dynamic, growing economies depend on their markets as an honest mechanism for change. In the sense that markets cannot function effectively without government protections and enforcements, a laissez-faire political economy is an oxymoron. Effective discharge of governmental responsibilities presupposes possession of resources with which to meet their obligations—this means taxing authority. Any society wishing to employ markets as its change mechanism to grow and prosper must reach a consensus on the government policies that will appropriately support the effective operation of its markets.

In addition to protecting market operations from unfair behavior or influence, governments have the Solomon-like assignment of achieving a standard of equity among its citizens. Without maintaining a politically acceptable equity standard, societies would be unable to develop stable relationships and institutions, including fair markets. The American standard of equity has traditionally been based on the concept of providing equal opportunity to all its citizens, not equal outcomes. However, some minimal level of income must be made available to all through government transfer programs (welfare, social security, and unemployment insurance). There should also be a progressive (higher tax rates as taxable income rises) federal income tax system, with the highest rates set at nonconfiscatory levels so that citizens will always be encouraged to earn additional income. Those who bristle at the thought of progressive (or any) taxes should consider that (1) government must have resources to carry out its role in the market system, and (2) it is senseless to levy taxes whose yield is less than collection costs, i.e., very low incomes are not worth taxing. Consequently, any tax that is not structurally regressive to income must be progressive. The concepts are readily apparent, but translating them into policy is much another matter.

This general framework describes the factors that have been considered in defining America's standard of equity. The body politic has and will continue to debate the specifics of what are equitable transfer payments for the poor, the retired or the disabled, and the unemployed, what various income groups should pay in federal taxes (recently, who should get what back in tax cuts), and how government should ensure all citizens equal opportunity, including the issue of health care that is the primary subject of this book. It is argued that market reforms of private health insurance would enhance our standard of equity by improving the opportunity of all Americans to obtain equal access to more efficiently delivered health care services.

Government has key roles to play in society, including policing the marketplace to keep it honest, fair, and safe. However, in the United States, the public sector has been outperformed by the private sector in bringing benefits to citizens. Both political parties need to be more pro-government in the sense of making it work better. Democrats often expect too much and settle for too little in the way of performance, while many Republicans just want it to go away; neither approach has been very helpful in terms of making government more efficient or more service oriented. Nevertheless, the United States has been fortunate in that Americans have generally been quite skeptical about the ability of government to solve their economic problems. Its representative government has respected that skepticism because Americans are generally self-reliant and freedom-loving. Never, even in the depth of the Great Depression, have Americans, except for farmers, been willing to sacrifice their independence for government programs that promise to ease to their economic burdens. As a consequence, the challenge of balancing governmental activities with the operation of an effective free market has not been as difficult in the United States as in most of the rest of the world. The contrast with other nations' lack of opportunity and reluctance to accommodate new alternatives is still strongly rooted here. Even our continuing debates about the equity of specific tax and transfer payment programs have generally been conducted within the context of their likely effects on the operation of a free market. Americans have, indeed, been fortunate, but continued vigilance will be required.

IDEOLOGICAL DIVIDES

Different views of equity figure very prominently in the ideological disputes over the passage of national or universal health insurance, which is typically described as a battle over entitlements. However, it is certainly not the only area of dispute. We have already noted the major disagreement over the role of markets in health care delivery and financing. The other principal dispute is over the issue of taking any action at all to significantly change the status quo in health care. As has been pointed out in Chapter 1 and in our discussion about the nature of government, there has been a great reluctance since 1965 for Congress to take any major steps toward reforming America's health care system, with the exception in 2003 of adding a pharmaceutical benefit to the Medicare program, which barely meets the definition of reform. It is always easier for entrenched interest groups to block any legislative reform by attacking the unknown effects of proposed new programs in comparison to all the known benefits of the existing system. Thus far, that defense has successfully repelled any attempt to reform the nation's health care system, and it will be the toughest obstacle to overcome in passing significant health care reform in the 21st century. Each of these three ideological divides will be discussed in this section, starting with the toughest issue facing reformers of either stripe.

Defending the Status Quo in Health Care

Getting a majority of Congress to support federal health insurance legislation is the biggest hurdle facing health care reform. A lot of conservatives in both parties are ideologically opposed to either national or universal health insurance because they do not want to expand the federal government's programmatic activities or, more important, its expenditure budget and, thus, have to raise taxes. It is this group of bipartisan fiscal conservatives that will utilize (and be used by) special interests in the health care industry to defend the status quo in health care and defeat any major new federal intrusion into their affairs. The health lobby is typically the highest spending of all sector lobbies, with both the American Medical Association and the American Hospital Association included in the ten largest lobbying organizations [Mullins]. There will be a lot of lobbying pressure exerted against federal health insurance if these organizations dig in their heels in opposition to NHI or UHI. There can be little doubt that the health insurance lobby's ad campaign against the Clinton health reform plan was one of the most significant factors in persuading public opinion to oppose the Clinton plan.

The primary question is: what positions will the health-industry lobby take on the single-payer NHI or income-related catastrophic UHI plans? Virtually the entire health lobby will be opposed to single-payer NHI because it is so threatening to their self-interests. The health insurance carriers will uniformly oppose single-payer approach as defined in HR676, their legislative proposal, for the most obvious reason that it would put them all out of business. Similarly, the pharmaceutical industry will vehemently oppose the federal price-setting mechanism for drugs, and it is likely that the American Medical Association will also oppose the fee regulation in HR676, even though the plan was developed by a group of physicians, but these physicians are much more liberal than the views of the average AMA member, and the plan fully supports fee-for-service practice, the cherished principle of the medical profession. Many of the physician specialty groups, like the pathologists and radiologists, will also oppose the elimination of for-profit enterprises prominently advocated in the single-payer approach. Hospital and nursing home associations are also likely to oppose HR676 because of opposition to governmental budgeting as the only route for earning revenues. In other words, the whole health lobby is likely to come down hard against the single-payer, governmental plan.

On the other hand, although most of these same health care and insurance organizations would rather maintain the status quo than support an income-related catastrophic UHI proposal, they would willingly participate in legislative discussions of UHI and provide suggestions for amendments that could make the price competition more compatible with their own self-interests. Make no mistake about it, though, to the extent that health care providers and insurers understand how much different it will be to practice under full-scale price competition, the less enthusiastic will be their support of UHI, even though all of these groups have fully supported private markets in their past opposition to other health insurance proposals. And the health insurers have the matter of their own survival. Under no circumstances would the health lobby become an enthusiastic supporter of UHI unless they believed that the passage of some form of federal health insurance was imminent. The health lobby would most likely view UHI as the lesser of two evils.

The matter of self-interest concerning federal health insurance certainly, however, extends beyond the health lobby. Businesses, currently the second highest (to the federal government) payer for health care provided in the United States, has but one real bottom line interest in the legislative consideration of federal health insurance: maximize the amount of the transfer for the liability of health insurance from businesses to government and, thus, maximize the reduction in labor costs from health insurance legislation. In the case of continued labor costs, the proposed payroll tax in HR676 on all employees of 3.3 percent that will have to be paid by businesses, while less than businesses currently pay on average for employee health insurance, is likely to be higher than the costs UHI supporters, who look primarily to income taxes for health insurance financing, are likely to ask of business. In addition, businesses are philosophically attracted to the market competition theme emphasized by UHI supporters. Nevertheless, businesses, as supporters of some form of federal health insurance, will be actively involved in negotiations over the health insurance legislation and could well be in play to support either approach for the right proposal for financing the insurance. The single-payer supporters may wish to reconsider the sources of financing they recommend in exchange for support of some or most of the powerful business lobby.

With businesses actively supporting federal health insurance legislation, the prospects of maintaining status quo in health care becomes seriously diminished and the biggest hurdle in the passage of some form of federal health insurance may have been overcome; despite all those who thought just over 12 years ago after the Clinton debacle that federal health insurance would never be passed in the United States. The possibility of passing any federal health insurance legislation will change the whole tenor the debate. It suggests that the health lobby, with or without enthusiastic support, will have to throw itself behind UHI legislation and begin to bargain for the best deal it can get, just to stop the single-payer NHI bill. And it further suggests that the remaining ideological differences are likely to come into increased prominence in the legislative debate over federal health insurance.

Nevertheless, there will be other interest groups, such as organized labor, various consumer organizations, and the baby boom generation, that, in terms of their self interests, will support the single-payer approach and oppose income-related catastrophic coverage. The baby boomers are the most obvious opponents of catastrophic coverage because it will mean lesser Medicare benefits than previous generations of seniors have received. Labor unions will oppose taxing employee fringe benefits; tax free employee benefits literally built unions in this country in the post World War II period. And consumer groups have traditionally been suspicious of market mechanisms and are generally supportive of the single-payer advocate's argument that health care should be available to patients without cost sharing.

The Appropriate Health Care Entitlement

Probably no ideological issue will be more seriously debated then the definition of the new health care entitlement. Indeed, debate over this issue is likely to be given greatest prominence to the public while Congress debates the intricacies of the issue. Will the public favor a full scale social insurance program with equal and full coverage for all Americans or will the social insurance be limited to full comprehensive coverage for lower income Americans and income-related catastrophic coverage for all Americans who are financially able to pay some or all of their costs? When the question is asked, most polls indicate that about 80 percent of Americans agree that access to health care should be a right, but there is a great deal of confusion about whether that includes federal government financing to ensure access. Some 62 percent of the most recent Gallup poll (November 2002) favored universal coverage of all Americans by the federal government, but that doesn't indicate that everyone should have the same coverage or whether the public is prepared to pay increased taxes to support a program of equal comprehensive coverage. What do the voters think will be fair and affordable?

Currently, what is fair depends very much on the kind of insurance that citizens obtain for health services. Stone [1993] has contrasted the underlying definition of fairness in private and social insurance. The fairness of private insurance is judged actuarially: the premium rates should correspond to the expected risk of loss for the individual or group purchasing the insurance. In contrast, the fairness of social insurance is judged by a sharing of risk across the community or market in question, what Stone describes as the solidarity principle in which mutual assistance is provided to all members of the community. Will those citizens at lesser risk willingly pay higher rates to assist those who, often through no fault of their own, have greater risk? But even with that question unanswered, Stone's definition also falls short of answering the question about how much of the risks needs to be spread.

Is it fair to share only the risks of catastrophic illness across the entire nation or must we share the costs of all health care risks nationally, as the full social insurance advocates argue. Conservatives believe that it is inappropriate for government to do things for citizens that they can afford to do for themselves, part of the conservative maxim about individual responsibility to the extent able. As a consequence, the conservative definition of appropriate social insurance is to only share the risks of health care costs that are unaffordable for families. For the low income families, that is all health care costs, but for higher income families, it may be very little because they can afford to pay most or all of their own health care costs. The conservative approach seems to be consistent with the American standard of equity that provides all Americans with equal access to more efficiently delivered health care services, because there can be little doubt that a reformed health care market that is price competitive will be much more efficient than a governmentally operated health care system.

In the final analysis, the American choice of how much social insurance is enough to achieve American justice in health care will be up to the voters who will be bombarded by public advertising from both sides. My guess is that public opinion will fluctuate back and forth over the entire time Congress is debating the legislation in response to especially appealing advertisements from either side, because American public opinion is anything but ideological—it's pragmatic and fickle. However, in the end American skepticism about government operation of complex programs like health care is likely to favor market reform over a single-payer plan. Income-related catastrophic health insurance is favored to be the victor in the public debate over how much government assistance is needed to create reasonably equitable access to health care for all Americans. It will, nevertheless, be an extremely interesting public policy debate to observe.

The Adequacy of Markets in Health Care

The predicted outcome in the social insurance debate favoring UHI is largely dependent on persuading Americans that a reformed health care market will, indeed, overcome the deficiencies that have been observed over the years. In addition, the recent Part D Medicare pharmaceutical program caused a great deal of consternation among seniors both because of the complexity of market choices that were made available and the large number of administrative problems and delays many seniors had in initially registering for the drug benefit. However, that experience is really a two-edged sword, for market advocates will blame government administrators for the chaotic registration process, while at the same time the pro-government advocates will cite the complexity and confusion in making market choices about pharmaceutical distributors, almost suggesting that it would be better and easier to have government make the choices for you. The program made a serious mistake in not limiting the number of alternative drug distributors to a smaller number of choices, while assuring that the various types of distribution approaches were represented. The one significant lesson learned from the recently developing behavioral economics discipline is that too many choices can quickly overwhelm a rational decision-making process [Schwartz et al], as it did in this case.

But in addition to the public relations debate about the Medicare drug program, there will eventually be real information on how effectively the market competition operated to reduce the cost of pharmaceuticals. So far, the limited experience suggests that the cost of program will be significantly lower than originally estimated because of the lower than expected cost of pharmaceuticals [Pear]. If the fuller experience of the program bears out this finding, it will help answer one of the fundamental issues that separates the two approaches in buying health care services. The single-payer advocates argue that government negotiators, employing monopsonistic buying techniques, can drive a better bargain than competitive markets can achieve. The Medicare drug experience may well provide empirical information to settle this dispute.

However, the real villains in the public's view from their past health care market experiences have been health insurance companies (including the Blues) and all sorts of managed care companies (including HMOs) who were given the tough job of saying no to consumers during the ascendancy of managed care competition in the '90s. Health insurance companies were always suspect in consumers' minds probably because the public recognized that they didn't provide much value for the premiums they received. However, managed care organizations found themselves in the unenviable role of being between the physicians, who wanted to do something to help patients and their employers who wanted to save money by eliminating unnecessary medical care. It was an impossible assignment and the employers quickly gave up to worker pressure and rescinded all the effective controls that were, in fact, saving employers money through more efficacious care. The only residual effect of the managed care revolution of the '90s has been the tarnished image of health insurance companies and managed care organizations.

As a consequence, the toughest sell to the public that the reformed health care market will be more effective is to persuade consumers that those old villains, insurance companies and managed care organizations, are now going to become their advocates and provide advice on how to get the medically best and most economical health care. The assignment for health insurers and managed care organizations is to quickly bridge the gap during the course of the congressional debate to convince the public that they can do their new assignment effectively and perform a real service for consumers that will result in better and less expensive health care. We can expect health insurers and managed care organizers to make every effort possible, for the stakes for them will be extremely high—a second chance or extinction. The success of UHI legislation is dependent upon persuading enough of the public that income-related catastrophic coverage really will transform the health care market into an efficient, effective, and equitable means of delivering and financing health care for all Americans.

PRACTICAL POLITICS

As was noted in the first chapter, conservatives have the legislative advantage on the federal health insurance issue. They have prevented the passage of health insurance for 90 years and counting, sometimes with inaction as they did in preventing President Roosevelt in the '30s from even introducing a plan or with an active campaign as they did most recently in shooting down the Clinton plan. Should conservatives introduce and actively support UHI legislation in the 111th (2009-10) Congress, it would totally change the tenor of the debate and would move the nation much closer than it ever has been to the enactment of a federal health insurance program.

Historical Precedence

Having support by both major parties for federal health insurance would not be unprecedented. In the early 1970s both parties introduced health insurance legislation—Presidents Nixon and Ford introduced employer-mandated health insurance proposals, Senator Edward Kennedy introduced a single-payer, governmental health insurance proposal, and Senator Russell Long of Louisiana even introduced a catastrophic insurance plan in a Congress that was heavily-dominated by Democrats. Both Nixon and Ford were, however, considered moderates and the more conservative Republican members of Congress did not fully support their efforts, but it didn't matter because the air quickly went out of the health insurance balloon when huge cost overruns were reported for the first years of the Medicare program, which illustrates the effect on utilization that can occur when the price of medical care is dropped significantly. Congress then took up legislative reform of the Medicare program to stem its cost problems, with the first post-Medicare amendment of the Social Security Act being passed in 1972 and Congress spending most of the remainder of the decade debating other types of cost controls. Trying to figure out how to control health care costs became such a Herculean effort that Congress did not seriously take up federal health insurance for all

Americans again in Congress until 1993 when President Clinton introduced his employer-mandated plan. Congress never did figure out how to control health care costs. The market only successfully contained hospital and physician costs through managed care in the '90s until employees revolted and got employers to back down on the program's most effective regulations.

The significant difference between 2009 and the early '70s is the likelihood of serious support by the business lobby for some form of federal health insurance. Although the business lobby did not actively oppose employer-mandated coverage when it was considered earlier, it did oppose the Clinton plan in 1994. All out active support for federal health insurance by the business lobby would, indeed, be precedential, would change the tenor of the debate, and virtually assure its passage by bringing, for the first time, significant conservative support for federal health insurance. Under such circumstances, the wheeling and dealing in Congress could become quite unpredictable with various members of Congress trying to make a name for themselves. It should be fun to watch, for the twists and turns in the legislative process could be very intriguing for Congress will not be constrained as this book has been in only analyzing only two extreme possibilities. The number of items on which some form of compromise can be made is very large.

The Make Up of the 111th Congress

In the speculation about the actions of a future Congress, wouldn't the likely outcome of the legislative debates of the 111th (2009-10) Congress be greatly influenced by the outcome of the 2008 elections? The answer to this obvious question is: probably not unless the number of left-of-center Democrats increased substantially. The Democrats have controlled, by varying margins, all of the Congresses that have seriously considered federal health insurance and there has always been a sufficiently large number of conservatives or less extreme liberals in the make up of the Democratic majorities to preclude passage of health insurance legislation. The 2008 presidential and congressional elections will, however, be important, partly because the type of health insurance will be one important issue in determining the outcome of those elections. If one party successfully campaigns on either NHI or UHI, it will surely give that party a leg up when the 111th Congress convenes. Capturing the presidency will also influence the federal health insurance debate, but a winning centrist Democratic president is as likely to support UHI as NHI.

In the final analysis, it is the ideological make up of the 111th Congress and the ideology of the new president, not the winning political party, will be the crucial determinant of the kind of federal health insurance that is likely to emerge. Unless liberals win a landslide victory in 2008, which in light of the current closeness of the political divide in America is unlikely, there will be a sufficiently large enough conservative-to-moderate majority in Congress to favor UHI. Universal health insurance is the smaller legislative change to the status quo: all the existing players in the delivery and financing of health care continue to participate; the purchase of health insurance (for those who choose to buy insurance coverage) will continue to be at place of employment, which is favored by 75 percent of Americans [Kaiser], even if the dollars spent will now be the employee's and not the employer's and the change in the federal budget will be smaller. Because there is underlying and fundamental American suspicion about the economic effectiveness of government, it will be much easier to pass UHI than NHI. As the next section outlines, UHI is the hands-down favored bipartisan compromise without even knowing who will be elected to the 111th Congress or who the 46th President of the United States will be.

KNITTING TOGETHER A
BIPARTISAN COMPROMISE

One way to test the ideological viability of the income-related catastrophic proposal is to compare its characteristics with the lessons learned from the nation's 90 years of legislative experience with federal health insurance. The first lesson is to recognize that conservatives have an instinctive opposition toward all health insurance proposals because of their native skepticism about the role of government. Conservatives are unlikely to support health insurance unless there are special extenuating circumstances or features of the plan that permit the advancement of other conservative objectives, like ensuring the balancing of the budget by reducing the net cost of federal health entitlements.

As was noted in Chapter 1, the history of federal health insurance legislative failures also indicates that bipartisan support of both liberals and conservatives is necessary for its passage. A useful way to interpret health insurance legislative history is as a negative-iterative process. For the past 90 years liberals and moderates have proposed federal health insurance plans, and the Congress has in turn discarded them, primarily due to objections from conservatives. These failed proposals provide a means for gradually eliminating all but the few that just might meet the conservatives' objections—negative iteration to discover the possible successful proposals.

What's Left?

The '90s debate over the Clinton plan and then the Republicans' attempt to reform existing health entitlements has been prodigious in discarding options, and much can be learned from that legislative history for developing a compromise federal health insurance bill. The following lessons can be learned from those deliberations about the properties of a passable federal health insurance plan:

1. The fairly liberal 103rd (1993-94) Congress' opposition to the regulatory apparatus proposed by President Clinton—coupled with the conservative successes in the 1994 and subsequent congressional elections—suggests that any health insurance proposal that seeks to control health care costs through economic regulation will have difficulty in getting approved.

2. In the final analysis, business could not support a government mandate of the employer model in the Clinton plan and business

is likely to actively campaign to eliminate or at least reduce its obligation for employee health benefits. As a consequence, a government mandate of the employer health insurance model is dead, despite the recent Massachusetts miracle.

3. Without an employer mandate, the only way to finance additional coverage for the uninsured population is new federal taxes, which was the avoidance strategy for conservative support of mandated insurance. Both the current federal budget situation and the experience of the moderate Senate incremental reformists in the 103rd Congress suggest that the insurance benefits will have to be scaled back from the low-dollar comprehensive coverage that has been considered in previous congressional plans. A comprehensive set of low-dollar benefits simply costs too much. Further, it is unacceptable to conservatives who believe that citizens should be financially responsible for their economic behavior to the extent that they are financially able. In addition, the size of the tax increase necessary to finance universal first-dollar comprehensive coverage and the denial of financial responsibility to the able would be politically impossible for conservatives to support.

4. Even though the GOP attempts at Medicare reform in the 104th (1995-96) Congress, the first Republican controlled congress in generations, did not arguably endanger or hurt aged Americans entitled to health insurance benefits, the lesson of that Congress is that the Medicare program should not be changed for its existing beneficiaries, unless some of those beneficiaries wish to voluntarily participate in the new program. The issue is simply too sensitive, and thus too politically exploitable. Federal health insurance can still be used as a method of redefining the federal health entitlements, but it must be done prospectively with the new program being implemented for persons reaching 65 at some future date.

5.   The lesson of the 104th Congress' budget debacles when government was shut down for the longest time in its history is that one of the few ways to gain conservative support for a health insurance plan in the near-term is to reduce the federal government's net cost of health care entitlements in a manner that is less self-serving to government than its current negotiated-price purchasing policy. The rising number of Medicaid recipients suggests that government cannot continue to ignore the rising numbers of uninsured people in the future cost of existing federal health entitlements.

A federal program of income-related catastrophic coverage could be designed to meet all five of these criteria. That is, the income-related catastrophic proposal would require little government regulation of the health care market; it would eliminate all employer-insurance mandates and freeze the employers' cost of health benefits at current levels; the plan represents the most reasonable or affordable cost of health insurance coverage to the federal government of any health insurance plan; it would provide a fair transition from existing entitlements; and, it would reduce the federal government's net cost of existing health entitlements while totally eliminating state governments' health financing obligations over a five-year period. In summary, the plan is responsive to all the problems and objections that have been raised in the '90s debate over macro health reform and Medicare reform in the 103rd and 104th Congresses.

Further, it offers a basis for bipartisan agreement between conservatives and liberals on health reform. It appeals to conservatives as a way of reforming the health insurance market by reversing the emphasis in insurance from first-dollar to last-dollar coverage to constrain the nation's health care cost increases. For liberals, the most attractive aspect of universal catastrophic benefits is the application of a social insurance concept, which not only makes a veto unlikely by a Democratic president but could also attract Democratic congressional support. Every American (or resident alien), in accordance with financial need and with those in poverty being eligible for first-dollar coverage, would gain the security of having a portable, non-cancelable health insurance benefit that serves as the base for planning the purchase of needed health care. Last-dollar coverage will also correct the existing deficiencies in the insurance market that cause higher-risk persons to have difficulty in obtaining private insurance coverage.

Members of either political party will want to participate in an effort to bridge the longstanding policy schism only if they are confident about the validity of their own party's ideologies on health care. These ideologies have guided the parties' positions in this debate and an understanding, at the outset, that the bottom line position in these negotiations must be the passage of a UHI plan sufficiently consistent with fundamental beliefs of both parties. As part of this commitment, party members must recognize that once enacted, subsequent amendments will be needed to correct the plan's operating deficiencies. The bipartisan supporters of this effort must believe that the program's shortfalls will be consistent with their party's remedial approaches while knowing that the other party's participants believe equally strongly that subsequent amendments will support their ideology. For liberals and conservatives to reach agreement, each side must believe fundamentally in the future vision of its own ideology.

Because of their skepticism about government, it is harder for conservatives than liberals to initiate a health insurance proposal. That is why the easiest and surest way to succeed is to obtain at the outset Republican leadership support for such a proposal. The Republican plan will, naturally, be built on a platform of market reform that will result in private parties making most decisions without government coercion. However, the participating Republicans must understand the government's financing and tax role to overcome limitations that have led to shortfalls in the equity of market results and the operating efficiency of the health care market. Neither the market nor government can wholly succeed in resolving the nation's health care problems without a mutually productive relationship for both entities.

Nevertheless, a number of substantive issues need to be understood and accepted before this proposal can serve as the basis for a bipartisan initiative to solve the health entitlements budgetary problem through the enactment of UHI. Each of these issues represents a potential challenge that could derail the initiative. The issues will be presented in order of significance, and, where possible, related findings from public opinion surveys will be cited to indicate how voters are likely to react to specific aspects of the proposal.

The Tax Challenge

Whether the popularity of government support for health care is greater than the unpopularity of tax increases is the most controversial question in evaluating the UHI alternative for balancing the budget. The program could largely be financed by making employer health insurance premium contributions taxable for individuals. Such a tax change is undoubtedly the major political obstacle for the proposal's acceptability. However, approximately a one-third savings in the cost of private health insurance would more than offset any net increase in taxes. For most Americans that goes a long way toward diminishing the political negatives of the tax change. In addition to the cash savings in premiums, the protection of last-dollar coverage will encourage many consumers to reexamine the kind and level of other health insurance coverage they will need. Healthier families may wish to self-insure below the federal coverage and put funds aside in liquid assets to finance medical emergencies (the HSA approach). Higher-risk persons who currently have difficulty in obtaining private insurance coverage should no longer have a problem in obtaining low-dollar coverage and at a much lower cost.

Nevertheless, tax changes are subject to sloganeering, and it may be difficult for many workers to understand that their net take-home pay will increase because their insurance costs will decrease more than their taxes will increase. For Republicans there is the additional risk of apparently violating their credo that the party would enact no new taxes. So, even though take-home pay for the average worker and nearly all two-worker families with employer-sponsored insurance will rise, individual Republicans would have to evaluate whether the damage from raising costs and/or reducing choice for the aged is greater than the tax flak that will be generated. It should also be noted that, if enough Republicans are willing to accept this risk, it represents the strongest argument that the Republicans really are committed to a bipartisan UHI effort—their admission ticket, so to speak.

Fortunately, health care ranks very high in the public's priorities—tied for third among the highest ranking issues facing Congress (right after "War in Iraq" and the economy, and tied with "Terrorism/National Security") according to a Kaiser Family Foundation/Harvard School of Public Health November 2004 poll [2005]. Within the health care agenda, the public, by that same poll, ranks: "lowering the cost of health care and insurance, making Medicare more financially sound for the future, and increasing the number of Americas with insurance," as the three highest priorities. In addition, 45 percent of those polled were willing to pay higher premiums or taxes to increase the number of insured Americans versus 51 percent who were opposed to paying higher anything to meet that goal. The idea that a public relations campaign over the tax changes and making financially-able citizens pay for affordable lower dollar health insurance through their employers in order to obtain income-related catastrophic coverage certainly seems plausible from this polling information.

There is, nevertheless, a negative aspect to this change in the tax treatment of employee health insurance benefits. Labor unions and some more-liberal congressmen are ideologically opposed to any taxation of employment benefits. Former Senator Bob Packwood, for example, in the 1986 tax reform deliberations almost single-handedly kept the issue off the tax reform agenda. This is a fundamental ideological issue because economic conservatives believe just as strongly that the tax exemption, by encouraging excessive insurance coverage, has been a major contributing factor in U.S. health care inflation. Although efforts should be made to persuade the labor unions that this change will enhance choice and increase take-home pay for their members, it is probably best to simply recognize this aspect of the issue cannot be compromised in a market-oriented health care reform proposal. The elimination of the tax exemption is central to the development of consumer incentives for cost conscious behavior.

The First Dollar Coverage Challenge

Another ideological difference between market-oriented reformers and more liberal reformers is the issue of first-dollar comprehensive coverage, including preventive care like vaccinations and health screenings. Liberals argue that there should be no financial barriers in health insurance to obtaining necessary care. Therefore, almost all federal health insurance proposals have included very low deductibles and service fee copayments. In contrast, the income-related catastrophic plan has higher deductibles and copayments based on the consumer's ability to pay as measured by family income, in order to make consumers cost conscious about purchasing health care services. This too represents an ideological or philosophical difference on which no compromise is possible, and is critical to improving the health market's efficiency.

It may, however, cause some apprehension among the public that since World War II has become accustomed to first-dollar coverage and free choice of physicians. Part of the reason health care is so expensive in the United States is that so many consumers have been able to obtain whatever health care they want without much out-of-pocket cost. There was much lower tension between buyers and sellers in the health care market than in other markets. As the managed care episode in the '90s demonstrated, that tension encourages sellers to lower their costs so that more of their products will be sold and causes buyers to consider their purchases in terms of the limit that it imposes on the quantities of other goods and services that they can buy.

The market reform proposal seeks to create some market tension in the purchase of health care services. It also seeks to ensure that all Americans can afford all needed health care services by assisting in the financing of affordable (based on family income) services through loan guarantees and by making government responsible for all unaffordable services, the catastrophic coverage. Nevertheless, some of the public will be concerned about this change in the method of financing health care services, and some congressional liberals will object to this prospective change in the federal health entitlement for the aged and the disabled. Public education should mediate the public's concern; the liberals' objection can be muted by pointing out that the poorest aged and disabled will actually obtain better benefits in the market reform plan than the current Medicare and Medicaid programs, with no additional out-of-pocket costs. More affluent persons who turn 65 after the plan is implemented will, however, have a larger personal liability for their health care services than under current Medicare benefits, but it should be a liability that they can afford, even if it is never politically popular to have to pay more—the most insidious difficulty with middle-class entitlements is the difficulty in rescinding them. Indeed, it may be more difficult politically to reform Medicare than to pass UHI because of the outcries of the baby boomers that will be the first generation to have to assume higher out-of-pocket costs than the current Medicare beneficiaries. Chapter 5 will demonstrate the financial reasons for the federal government for the necessity of implementing this change to federal health entitlements.

The Regulatory Challenge

Another fundamental difference between the two ideologies is the degree of confidence in the operation of the free market by conservatives in contrast to the liberals' view that government regulation of markets is needed to protect consumers. Clinton's unwillingness to abandon the health alliances and price controls, which cost his plan the support of all major segments of business, was in large part responsible for the decision of the business lobby to withdraw its support from the Clinton proposal. Without business support, the Clintons' efforts were viewed as a liberal approach to UHI, and general public support soon dissipated.

The free market in health care has not performed very effectively throughout most of this century—that is the central reason for advocating a market reform proposal. Recently price competition among health care providers was briefly intensified as a result of managed care coverage. Managed care did not, however, encourage consumers to actively seek lower-cost forms of health care or even evaluate the efficacy of care in a free market nor cheerfully accept the "managed" care decisions of others, because they received no personal advantage from the health care savings. Consumers must be directly rewarded for prudent decisions and penalized for poor economic choices for market reform to be effective.

The reform proposal does, indeed, reward and penalize health care consumers for the economic appropriateness of their behavior, and long before they are involved in making stressful decisions about health care options for themselves and their loved ones. The demand for health care will reflect the tension that arises from the recognition that more spent on health care means less will be available for other goods and services. Even though conservative economists are confident that these incentives will reform the health care market so that it operates as effectively as other private markets, skeptics will remain dubious.

The proposal seeks to overcome this and other ideological differences by allowing state governments to experiment with alternative programs so that evidence of effectiveness can be obtained on issues such as the use of market versus regulatory controls. The proposal includes broad authority to approve several different types of state experiments with both the financing and regulation of health care delivery as long as free and relatively unregulated competition is also given a fair trial in the majority of the states. The purpose of this experimentation is both to benchmark the effectiveness of unconstrained competition and to avoid the colossal errors that have sometimes marked major federal program interventions and entitlements.

Managed competition with the mandated purchase of health insurance by individuals would be an excellent experiment that perhaps Massachusetts and Washington would like to undertake. Other states, perhaps Vermont and Hawaii, may want to experiment with the single-payer, full social insurance approach to UHI. As long as the experimenting states develop a protocol that protects their residents' federal catastrophic benefits, protects the federal government from additional costs, and obtains the appropriate state legislative authorization for the remainder of the financing, the program should be very permissive to learn more about ways to provide more cost effective, efficacious health care in the United States. The period for this experimentation is most likely to occur at the end of a five-year transition period when states will be freed from their financial obligation for Medicaid. This certainly is a better way to learn than the process of negative iteration in the Congress that has been the learning process for UHI in the last 90 years. If skeptics of the market can persuade individual state governments that experimentation is appropriate to test their views on regulation or financing health insurance, broad authority should be granted to settle these ideological differences through actual demonstration and observation of which approach works better and what is more popular with voters.

In the final analysis, the enactment of an income-related catastrophic UHI has one other safety valve that could appeal to liberals favoring the single-payer NHI approach. If, as these liberals believe, the reform of the health care market will be unable to rein in health care costs, single-payer NHI could be enacted easily overtime by gradually increasing the income levels for those citizens who qualify for first-dollar coverage and simultaneously expand the regulatory apparatus to control health care costs. Moving to a full comprehensive health care benefit can be accomplished within the legislative framework established by income-related catastrophic UHI. Liberals could achieve their once in lifetime objective of a single-payer, government health care program by accepting UHI as the initial step in that process. After 90 years, it's time for liberals to bet the farm by accepting income-related catastrophic UHI as a possible first step toward single-payer NHI. If they are wrong and market reform does contain health care costs, no one is the loser. Indeed, all Americans finally win by getting the health care market back to its effective free market roots while making health care services financially available to all Americans.

BIBLIOGRAPHY

Kaiser Family Foundation/Harvard School of Public Health, "Health Care Agenda for the New Congress," January 2005.

Mullins, B., "U.S. Lobbying Hits a Record," *Wall Street Journal*, February 14, 2006.

Pear, R., "Federal Costs Dropping Under New Medicare Drug Plan, Administration Reports," *New York Times*, February 3, 2006.

Schwartz, B., Rose, H., and Snibbe, A.C., "Is Freedom Just Another Word for Many Things to Buy," *New York Times*, February 26, 2006.

Stone, D.A., "The Struggle for the Soul of Health Insurance," *Journal of Health Politics, Policy and Law*, Vol. 18 No. 3 (Summer 1993), pp. 287-317.

CHAPTER 5
The Future of Health Care in the United States

In this final chapter, we come full circle on *Mandate for 21st Century America*. In Chapter 1 we observed that the U.S. health care system is badly broken, and in contemplating the future of the American health care system, we see that the currently broken system will only get much worse in the future. Reform is the only hope for making health care in United States affordable, with equal access and higher patient safety standards in response to consumer demand. In this chapter, we first consider what will happen if the United States continues to operate its unreformed existing health care system. Then, we examine what America's health care system would be like if the federal government enacts in 2009 or 2010 UHI with income-related catastrophic health insurance. Not only are the cost savings to the nation significant in the effort to restore fiscal integrity, but the quality of American life could be substantially improved by giving everyone access to affordable, efficacious health care services as American free markets have delivered goods and services in the rest of the economy.

THE ABSURDLY HIGH COST OF DOING NOTHING

Usually forecasting is fraught with subjectivity and uncertainty, but forecasting the future of an unreformed American health care system is as close to a sure thing as a forecaster can ever find. Most of America's future in health care has already been determined; it's simply a matter of the demographics playing out. Most of the people who will live and incur health care costs in the first half of the 21st century have already been born and will live through a predictable pattern of diseases as they age. We also have nearly 50 years of experience with rising health care costs that, except for few years in 1990s when managed care briefly slowed down the rate of cost increases, has been unparalleled in its constantly rising rates of cost increases. Of course, there is always the possibility of some major break-through in medical research that will magically increase the rate of medical cures and dramatically reduce health care costs, but that likelihood is so small that it would be extremely unwise to pin our health policy hopes on such an event. As a consequence, we will proceed to an examination of future American health care costs if Congress and the President decide not to initiate health care reform. What will it cost Americans to maintain the status quo?

The principal driver of federal health entitlements in the 21st century is the aging of the American population, and the biggest increase in the number of aged (65 years old and older) will occur between now and 2030, when the baby boom generation reaches their full seniority, after which a smaller rate of increase in the number of aged will be experienced. Between 2010 and 2030, the number of aged is expected to increase from approximately 40 million aged persons to more than 71 million aged and the percentage of aged in the total population will rise from about 13 percent to nearly 20 percent. That's a big increase in the number of Medicare beneficiaries and a huge increase in the cost of federal health entitlements; the Congressional Budget Office (CBO) estimates the cost of federal entitlements for the aged (including Social Security) and Medicaid populations rising from the current 20 percent of the federal budget to about 30 percent in 2030, and rising 50 percent faster than the rest of the federal budget.

The problem with the CBO estimate is that it assumes that health care costs can be constrained to grow only 1 percent faster than the rate of growth in the GDP, but it doesn't include any reasons to make that low rate plausible. Historically, from 1970 to 2004 the rate of increase in health care costs has been 2.9 percent faster than the rate of growth in the GDP [CB0, 12/05]. Assuming even a 2.5 percent rate of cost increases, which is less than the historical average, it would increase total federal health care costs substantially higher than the CBO forecast, increasing costs by about 156 percent and bringing the cost of federal entitlements for the aged (including Social Security) and Medicaid to nearly 40 percent of the federal budget in 2030 at a rate 100 percent higher than the rate of increase in the rest of the federal budget.

The effect on the federal health budget of a one and half percent higher rate of growth in health care costs can be seen in Table 5.1, which compares just federal health expenditures to the nation's whole GDP. If the nation doesn't do something dramatic to control health care cost, by 2040, the federal government will be spending a greater percentage of GDP on just two health programs, Medicare and Medicaid, than the nation spent on all its health care programs in 2004. We simply cannot afford to continue our current federal health entitlements. The problem of health care entitlements is much more severe than the fiscal problems facing the Social Security program.

TABLE 5.1
Projected Federal Outlays for Health Programs
With Different Rates of Increase in Health Care Costs
As a Percentage of GDP for 2010 Through 2050

Year	Assuming A 1% Faster Growth Rate*			Assuming a 2.5% Faster Growth Rate*		
	Medicare	Medicaid	Total	Medicare	Medicaid	Total
2010	2.7	1.8	4.5	3.1	2.1	5.2
2020	3.6	2.3	5.9	5.3	3.4	8.7
2030	4.9	2.8	7.7	7.7	4.4	12.1
2040	6.0	3.4	9.4	10.9	6.2	17.1
2050	6.7	3.9	10.6	14.1	8.2	22.3

*Spending per enrollee grows 1 percentage faster than per capita GDP in the first set of projections and 2.5 percentage faster than per capita GDP in the second set of projections.
Source: CBO, "A 125-Year Picture of the Federal Government's Share of the Economy, 1950 to 2075," July 3, 2002.

As bad as the fiscal problems with health entitlements currently are, we need to think about how serious those problems would become if the current health entitlement were extended to all Americans without any copayments or deductibles, as the single-payer reform advocates recommend. Passage of HR676 would more than triple the number of federal beneficiaries and eliminate all copayments and deductibles, minimally an additional 10 to 12 percent in the federal government's share of health care expenses. It also suggests that, even if the single-payer approach incorporated copayments and deductibles as high as the current Medicare benefits, it would still be unaffordable. Thus, by 2030, even assuming the lower 1 percent rate of health care cost increases, the federal government's share for health care entitlements would be greater than 25 percent of GDP, and nearly 40 percent of GDP at the higher rate of cost increase. Without any copayments or deductibles, the latter, higher, estimate is the more likely. The United States simply cannot afford health care reform along the lines proposed by Himmelstein and Woolhandler—it would bankrupt the nation. It is absolutely essential that any health care reform the United States undertakes early in the 21st century must offer a plausible means for containing future health care costs.

COST SAVINGS OF UHI

Even though the existing system of health entitlements will produce some absurdly high costs over the next 24 years, the issue that must be discussed is: how will UHI legislation reduce those costs. There are primarily two sources: (1) the Medicare entitlement will be reduced by not offering full benefits to the approximately 60 percent of the Medicare beneficiaries that are in the middle (35 percent of the current beneficiaries) and high (25 percent) income groups; and (2) by reducing the rate of increase for health care costs, which is by far the more significant of the two factors. Each of the two factors will, in turn, be discussed after we review the experience of the current Medicare program.

Understanding Medicare and the Proposed Reform

We have a substantial body of information about the existing Medicare program. As Table 5.2 indicates we know almost precisely which Medicare beneficiaries are the most costly patients. Older Black chronically-ill institutionalized patients are, on average, likely to be the program's most expensive beneficiaries. In general, increasing age and the number of chronic conditions beneficiaries have tend to raise the average cost of health care for aged persons. And single greatest cost increase factor is whether the Medicare beneficiary is institutionalized or not; institutionalization increases Medicare costs more than 5.5 times, and many of these institutionalized beneficiaries also become eligible for Medicaid support, further increasing federal health care costs.

TABLE 5-2
Average Annual Cost for Medicare Beneficiaries
Age 65 and Over in 2001,
For Selected Characteristics

Selected Characteristics	Average Cost in Dollars
Race and Ethnicity	
White, not Hispanic or Latino	$11,032
Black, not Hispanic or Latino	13,081
Hispanic or Latino	8,449
Other	9,031
Total	10,946
Age	
65-74	$ 8,207
75-84	12,090
85 and Over	18,353
Institutional Status	
Community	$ 8,466
Institution	46,810
No. of Chronic Conditions	
None	$ 3,837
1 or 2	6,685
3 or 4	11,878
5 or more	15,784

Source: Centers for Medicare and Medicaid Services, Medicare Current Beneficiary Survey.

However, Table 5.3 considers the variable, beneficiary income, which is critical to modifying Medicare from a social insurance (equal benefits for all) to income-related catastrophic coverage (benefits according to ability to pay). Table 5.3 demonstrates, first, that lower income aged have higher health care costs than higher income aged (in

TABLE 5.3
Medicare Enrollee Average Health Care Costs
By Income Category
And Source of Payment for 2001

Annual Income	Health Costs	Govt. Share	Out-of-Pocket	Other*
Less than $10,000	$14,692	11,313 (77%)	$2,351 (16%)	$1,028 (7%)
$10,001-20,000	11,249	7,424 (66%)	2,362 (21%)	1,463 (13%)
$20,001-30,000	10,152	5,990 (59%)	2,436 (24%)	1,726 (17%)
$30,001 or more	8,855	4,693 (53%)	2,214 (25%)	1,948 (22%)

*Other payers include private health insurance, Department of Veterans Affairs, and other public programs.
Source: Centers for Medicare & Medicaid Services, Medicare Current Beneficiary Survey

general, better health is a function of education, which is also correlated with higher earnings), and, second, that, although the federal government pays a higher share of the lower income aged's health care costs (77 percent of total costs for lowest income aged to only 53 percent for the highest income aged), the dollar difference in out-of-pocket expenditures among income levels is slight (only $148 separates the highest amount of out-of-pocket expenses from the lowest and the higher income group (probably because of the purchase of supplemental health insurance) incurs the lowest amount of out-of-pocket expenditures for health care. This latter result may not be totally consistent with the social insurance advocates expectations when they campaigned for the social insurance concept to be incorporated into the original Medicare legislation in 1965. Indeed, when we considered the switchover of the Medicare program to income-related catastrophic coverage, the elimination of copayments and deductibles for those below 200 percent of the poverty level will substantially improve the financial condition of the poor aged person or household, just as the reform increases the out-of-pocket or health insurance premium costs

of those over 65 who can afford to pay a larger portion of their own health care costs. The proposed change in the Medicare entitlement is not social insurance, but it will improve the progressivity of the Medicare program; i.e., more lower-income American aged will received more health benefits while higher-income American aged received less. Having considered what we know about the existing Medicare program, we are now in a position to consider what would happen to federal health entitlement costs if the program were switched to income-related catastrophic health insurance coverage at some date in the future before the baby boomers reach seniority. Such a change would leave intact the current Medicare beneficiaries, except that lower income (200 percent of poverty level) aged would become eligible for a zero copay and deductible benefit. This improvement in benefits for lower income Americans, thus, increases the net cost of Medicare, but there are other changes that more than offset the cost of eliminating copayments and deductibles for low income aged currently in the Medicare program.

Table 5.4 provides a more differentiated income distribution of aged household incomes along with the percentage of households in each category in 2002 for our cost calculations. If we assume that income of

TABLE 5.4
Income Distribution of
Family Households Age 65 and Over
For 2002

Income Category	% of Aged Households		Cumulative %
Under $10,000	4.5%		4.5
$10,000-14,999	7.1%	Pov. $10,705	11.6
$15,000-24,999	20.9%		32.5
$25,000-34,999	19.6%	Med. $33,902	52.1
$35,000-49,999	18.4%		70.4
$50,000-74,999	15.3%		85.7
$75,000 and Over	14.3%		100.0

Source: U.S. Census Bureau, Department of Commerce

$20,000 or less a year qualifies for the elimination of out-of-pocket expenditures, then in 2002 approximately 7.6 million aged with an average annual out-of-pocket expenditure of $2,362 (the highest average for this income group from Table 5.3) would cost about $18 billion. However, raising the deductible to 10 percent of the recipients' family income in 2002 for the other 26.7 million Medicare beneficiaries would have reduced federal health entitlement costs by about $61.4 billion, and thus saving the federal government, net, $42.7 billion or 17.3 percent of the Medicare program's total operating cost in 2001. If the deductible were as high as 20 percent of family income, the net savings for the Medicare program would have been about $92.8 billion or 37.6 percent of Medicare's operating costs in 2001, but all current benefits for families with earnings of more than $30,000 would, on average, be eliminated. The calculation based on averages does not mean that some individuals experiencing catastrophic health care costs would not continue to receive benefits. These numbers have been derived from working with the average cost of Medicare beneficiaries for various income levels (Table 5.3) and can found in Appendix C at the end of this chapter. The appendix provides an approximate magnitude of the savings that can be generated by changing the entitlement formula. However, these are only rough estimates and Congress will have to engage insurance actuaries to calculate more precisely what the saving would have been for past years and, more important, what these savings are likely to be in future years in determining the appropriate benefits that the nation can afford and represents a fair set of benefits for new Medicare beneficiaries.

Applying this formula for cost savings to the baby boomer generation's future program expenditures is likely to provide even greater cost savings for the Medicare program because the coming generation is better educated, with likely higher retirement income, and perhaps even healthier than current seniors. These savings should ensure the solvency of the Medicare Trust Fund indefinitely into the future. In addition, many will argue that such a program of income-related entitlements is fairer than the existing social insurance type of benefits because beneficiaries pay according to their financial ability to pay. Lower income aged persons would receive a substantial increase in benefits and higher income aged will pay a much higher percentage of their health care costs. With such high health care costs, America can no longer afford to pay for middle-class entitlements.

Competitive Market's Health Care Cost Savings

As impressive as the cost savings of changing the health entitlement from equal benefits for all aged persons to income-determined benefits, this effect is only redistributing health care costs among different income groups and the federal government. The real source of cost savings to the American society will come from the power of effective price competition in driving down future rates of increases in health care costs, which can be partially accomplished by turning three-quarters of the new baby boomers into cost-minimizing, rational health care consumers, as they qualify for Medicare. We know from the experience in the 1990s with managed care that price competition among health care providers can at least keep health care cost increases in line with overall increases in the GDP as it did in six years from 1993 to 2000 [Levit et al]. The only way in which the health care market in those four years differed from the 51 other preceding years since World War II is that the administration of 86 percent of all private health insurance plan benefits was done through managed care organizations. As imperfect a means for bringing price competition of the health care market as managed care may be, it was, nevertheless, sufficient to hold health care cost increases to the general rate of growth in the nation's economy, as measured by its GDP.

The primary source of imperfection in managed care for bringing competition to the health care market was the failure to include direct benefits for the consumer. If we are going to expect consumers to embrace price competition in the health care market, they must share in the savings, an inducement for consumers' willing participation. All of managed care's savings went to the ultimate bill payer, the employer, and all that consumers got were distressing notices of the denial of care that their doctors had told them was needed. It is no small wonder that consumers (employees) revolted and employers had to find a method of producing cost savings in their health insurance benefits that is acceptable to their employees.

Alas, the only way employers can effectively reduce their liability for their employees' health insurance benefits in order to compete in global markets is to find another party to assume their social responsibility to their employees. The only possible source is the federal government. In addition, the federal government is the only entity that can restructure the health care and insurance markets in such a way that effective price competition can be brought to bear on the health care market. Restructuring the health care and insurance market will require starting all over again to eliminate the insurance problem of adverse selection and the consumer's problem with moral hazard. Only by having the federal government assume the insurance risk for catastrophic illness will noncatastrophic health care become insurable in the private insurance market, and only by having financially able consumers assume responsibility for their care to the extent that they are able can the moral hazard of health insurance be minimized. The most effective way for the federal government to provide these market corrections is through the enactment of an income-related catastrophic universal health insurance benefit.

The societal health care cost saving should exceed those derived from driving the rate of future health care cost increases to parity with growth in the overall economy, which was accomplished for the few years in which managed care programs were effective. We noted in Chapter 2 (page 60) that the savings estimate of having as much price competition in the hospital-doctor sector of the health care industry as the remainder of the health care industry had from 1950 to 1985 was somewhere between 24 and 30 percent, an amount that would explain why the United States spent so much more on health care than other developed nations. That amount of savings, 24 to 30 percent per year on hospital-doctor expenditures, seems to represent a reasonable goal for evaluating the new program. The saving from price competition in the health care market could easily exceed that goal because virtually all of the new technology that has been introduced since World War II in health care treatment regimes has been cost-increasing. Price competition should lead to the introduction of many more cost reducing technologies as competing providers try to find ways to reduce their prices in the health care market. Because cost-reducing technologies have been ignored for so long in American health care, there could be a period soon after the implementation in which the nation experiences substantial change in health care that drives health care costs down. However, such a cost-lowering period is not sustainable over the long haul because of the service nature of the health care industry—wages for health care workers and care givers are determined in the broader labor markets that reflect changes in overall productivity in American labor. Nevertheless, a price-competitive health care market will produce substantial cost savings that will make the earlier CBO future cost estimates appear absurdly pessimistic.

A price competitive market will compel health care providers to find the lowest cost alternative for providing any health service that consumers want and will value at an effective price. In a price competitive health care market, market participants, both providers and consumers, will have enough price and quality information for both parties to act rationally in purchasing and providing health care services. The objective of competitive markets is to make providers deliver value to consumers, its chief beneficiaries. The system's primary compulsion is to make providers search for innovative, lower cost ways of providing health services and/or to design new and better services while consumers are free to choose which and how many of these services they wish to purchase—the market's test of success. It's the innovative response of different competitors that will lead to the improved health care services and lower costs.

SUMMARY

Finally, a recapitulation of the argument for enacting universal health insurance is in order. We began by establishing that the American health care system is badly broken. The American health care system has three world records for inefficiency and inequity: it has the highest health care costs; it provides less accessibility to health care than any industrialized nation because of its fractured and inequitable health insurance system; and in addition, it has a poor patient safety record that subjects patients in America to greater risks than other industrialized nations. Even though American physicians practice the most technologically sophisticated medical care in the world, Americans do not have lower morbidity and mortality rates than other countries in the developed world. Consumers (voters) need to ask the question: why do Americans pay more, receive lesser quality care, and have so many citizens without any coverage at all?

We then asked the question of whether America's political system was up to the challenge of reforming America's health care delivery and financing system and concluded that the 2008 presidential and congressional elections offered a propitious opportunity for both parties to offer their ideological versions of how reform could be best undertaken. Two principal changes in the political landscape surrounding health care reform are occurring: first, global competition is eroding the ability of American business to finance health insurance for workers in this country, and second, the aging of America's population is making the nation's health entitlements unaffordable— we can no longer afford a middle-class health entitlement. Both of these political changes will put increasing pressure on conservatives who have blocked health care reform, except for Medicare and Medicaid, throughout the 20th century. Once conservatives recognize these changes, health care reform will be in play legislatively.

After quickly establishing that tinkering with the health care system cannot solve its systemic problems, we moved on to consider two major types of reform—a market-driven reform or a single-payer government reform system. The two prototypes of federal health insurance are based on either universal health insurance (UHI) or national health insurance (NHI) and are defined in Chapter 2. However, because UHI is based on reforming the health care market, we first analyzed the problems in the current health care market, noting the structural defects in the health insurance market and the lack of price competition in the health delivery system. The only exception occurred in 1990s when managed care organizations reached high enough market penetration to create some price competition among health care providers and the rate of increase in health care costs was briefly dampened. However, consumers, who were not rewarded by managed care (employers got all the benefits), revolted and competition again disappeared from the health care marketplace. The lack of price competition, together with an overemphasis on first or low dollar comprehensive health insurance coverage in employee health benefits, has created a most unusual market that is dominated by health care producers, specifically doctors and hospitals. The UHI proposal of providing free care to lower income Americans and income-related catastrophic health protection for all other Americans makes health care available to all. By linking federal health insurance to the financial ability to pay, middle class Americans will be forced to view health care like other goods and services in their budgets and, thus, consider the price of services in their choices. Consumer price sensitivity will instill price competition into the health care market and end producer domination of that market. Conversely, the NHI proposal would make the federal government totally responsible for all health care, abolish the private market for health care—including the abolition of all for-profit health care enterprises and health insurance companies, and provide free health care to all citizens.

The economic implications of the two different federal health insurance proposals were considered in Chapter 3. First, universal income-related catastrophic health insurance for all Americans above 200 percent of the family poverty level is shown to induce affluent Americans to take responsibility for financing their own family's care in same prudent manner they manage other purchases, but with a better knowledge and understanding brought about through their own medical and health care financing adviser. The resulting price competition in the health care market should create the same pressures for innovation and cost-saving that occurs in other sectors of the American economy. In addition, the health insurance market is reformed by making health insurers assume the risk for noncatastophic health care coverage, accountable to the federal government for each family's catastrophic benefits, and provide cost and medical information to families. The federal government becomes responsible for financing catastrophic health care coverage. The single-payer advocates' moral objections to health care markets are considered and found to be inconsistent with the fee-for-service payment mechanism permitted by the single-payer proposal. In addition, the single-payer approach's difficulties in making rational resource allocation in the health care and the problems of controlling excessive health care utilization raise serious concerns about the economic viability of the approach without the arbitrary rationing that has marked both the Canadian and British medical care systems. There can be little doubt that the reformed health care market of the UHI proposal is economically superior to the single-payer approach.

Chapter 4 considered the political viability of the two prototype reform proposals. Again the single-payer approach will face a much more difficult set of political hurdles, starting with the total opposition of health care delivery and financing organizations and the likely opposition of the business sector. The universal health care proposal represents a much more modest change than the NHI proposal. An analysis of the objections raised in recent congressional deliberations over federal health insurance shows that the UHI proposal overcomes the historical impediments to legislative action. The most difficult political problem in the UHI proposal is likely to come from the recommendation to modify Medicare benefits for the baby boom generation, which, as the final chapter makes clear, represents a means of restoring fiscal integrity to the federal government's health entitlement budget.

The final chapter assessed the financial implications of not reforming the health care system versus the costs in future tax increases of implementing a universal income-related catastrophic health insurance program. There are only two possible scenarios for American health care: either we do nothing and bankrupt the American economy with spiraling health care costs and a middle class entitlement that we cannot afford, or we enact income-related catastrophic universal health insurance that can control future health care costs and restore balance to the American economy. A single-payer, governmentally-operated health care system drops out of reform consideration, even if copayments as large as the current Medicare program were instituted, because its costs are significantly higher, or just as high, with the incorporation of copayments as the existing health entitlement that we can no longer afford. Thus, all that remains is the consideration of two possible futures: doing nothing or enacting UHI. The ball is now in Congress's court, and a sufficient number of conservatives and liberals must step forward, in a bipartisan sense of obligation to the nation, to finally mandate a universal health insurance program that can provide efficient, efficacious, and equitable health care for all Americans.

BIBLIOGRAPHY

Congressional Budget Office, The Congress of the United States, "The Long-Term Budget Outlook," December 2005.

"A 125-Year Picture of the Federal Government's Share of the Economy, 1950 to 2075," July 3, 2002.

Levit, K., Smith, C., Cowan, C., Lazenby, H., and Martin, A., "Inflation Spurs Health Spending in 2000," *Health Affairs*, Vol. 21, No. 1 (January/February 2002), pp. 172-181.

APPENDIX C

Calculations of Approximate Savings for Medicare Program Of Switching to Income-Related Catastrophic Coverage

Tables C.1 and C.2 provide the calculations of the approximate savings for the Medicare program of switching the existing Medicare benefits to an income-related catastrophic benefit of 10 or 20 percent, respectively, of the beneficiaries family income. Out of necessity, the calculations make two assumptions: first, the beneficiaries will continue to receive supplemental payments from private health insurance, Department of Veterans Affairs, and other public programs that paid part of the health care costs in 2001 (from Table 5.3) and, second, the income distribution of beneficiaries in 2001 is approximately the same as 2002 (from Table 5.4). For persons below 200 percent of the poverty level, which we have assumed to be $20,000 or less, the new program would have to pay all of their out-of-pocket expenditures of $2,362. As a consequence, in both examples, the federal government would have additional program expenditures of $18 billion for low income families, $2,363 times 7.6 million Medicare beneficiaries. The purpose of the calculations is simply to point out that savings could be derived by changing the Medicare entitlement from a social insurance program with equal benefits for all beneficiaries to benefits related to the financial needs of beneficiaries. The dollar amounts of the calculation are only intended to be rough estimates of the changes. More detailed actuarial studies would be required to obtain more precise estimates for Congress.

In the 10 percent deductible example, there would be in addition $700 million expenditure for families earning between $20,000 and $24,999. The $700 million estimate is obtained by subtracting the supplemental payments ($1,726) from the total health care costs of this income category, $10,152 (also from Table 5.3) and finding the net average health care expenditures of $8,426 and subtracting the deductible for this income group of $2,250. That would mean this group would incur health expenses of $6,176, which is $186 higher than the $5,990 than Medicare had been paying. Multiplying that $186 by the 7.6 million Medicare beneficiaries with family earnings less than $25,000 but more than $20,000 produces the $700 million in increased federal program costs.

Table C.1
Savings with a 10% Deductible
On Medicare Benefits

Family Income	No. of Benes	Deductibles	Change in Avg. O-of-P	Total Savings
$19,999 or less	7.6 mil.	0	($2,362)	($18.0 bil.)
$20K to $24,999	3.6 mil.	$2,250	($ 186)	($ .7 bil.)
$25K to $29,999	3.4 mil.	$2,750	$ 314	$ 1.1 bil.
$30K to $34,999	3.4 mil.	$3,250	$1,064	$ 3.5 bil
$35K to $49,999	6.3 mil.	$4,250	$2,036	$ 21.0 bil
$50K to $74,999	5.2 mil.	$6,250	$4,036	$ 12.8 bil
$75,000 & above	4.9 mil.	$7,500	$4.693	$ 23.0 bil.
Total	34.4 mil.			$ 42.7 bil.

Similarly, the next higher income group, which also had net health costs of $8,426 per beneficiary and an average federal cost of $5,990 but a deductible of $2,750, would have a new federal liability of $5,676 and would have produced a savings of $314 ($5,990-$5,676) or a savings of $1.1 billion to the federal government. The rest of the calculations for the remainder of income groups in Table C.1 are made in the same way, but the net health costs are $6,907, less the rising deductible for each succeeding income group, until $4,693 becomes the average out-of-pocket cost for families earning more than $75,000. That does not mean that individual families earning more than $25,000 with high catastrophic health costs would not have received Medicare benefits, but on average each of these income groups would receive lower payments, so that the averages represent a savings to the federal government over the existing Medicare program. In summary, families earning less than $25,000 would receive higher payments from the federal government, but families earning more than $25,000 would receive less in the way of Medicare benefits.

Table C.2 repeats these same calculations for a 20 percent deductible in the income-related catastrophic coverage, which would increase the out-of-pocket health care expenses, on average, for every family income group earning more than $20,000 and all of the net expenses for families earning more than $30,000 would, on average, be the responsibility of the families. Again this does not mean that some families earning more than $30,000 and with higher health care costs would be eligible for some Medicare benefits. The exercise was directed only at estimating the effect on the federal health entitlement of moving to an income-related catastrophic coverage for Medicare beneficiaries.

Table C.2
Savings with a 20% Deductible
On Medicare Benefits

Family Income	No. of Benes	Change in Deductibles	Avg. O-of-P	Total Savings
$19,999 or less	7.6 mil.	0	($2,362)	($18.0 bil.)
$20K to $24,999	3.6 mil.	$4,500	$2,064	$ 7.4 bil.
$25K to $29,999	3.4 mil.	$5,500	$3,064	$10.4 bil.
$30K to $34,999	3.4 mil.	$6,500	$4,693	$16.0 bil
$35K to $49,999	6.3 mil.	$8,500	$4,693	$29.6 bil
$50K to $74,999	5.2 mil.	$12,500	$4,693	$24.4 bil
$75,000 & above	4.9 mil.	$15,000	$4.693	$23.0 bil.
Total	34.4 mil.			$92.8 bil.

Consideration should also be made of having a lower deductible for the population aged 65 and over than the deductible that is charged for the under 65 population. That is, Congress might agree to a 10 percent deductible in calculating the income-related catastrophic for the 65 and over and a higher deductible for those under 65. However, this illustration does clarify what is being proposed as a universal health insurance benefit for the American people and the underlying conservative principle that, if people can afford to be responsible for their health care costs, they should be expected to pay their fair share, according to their ability to pay.

INDEX

prepayment 33, 39, 41-2, 49 90, 99, 102, 115; knowledge about 29, 47; markets 40, 47-8, 51, 55-7, 60, 63-4, 66, 69, 72-6, 81, 97-9, 101, 104-6, 108-9, 114-8, 123, 137-9, 145-6, 151-2, 162-7; decisions 103, 105; needs, necessary, or problems 27, 39, 76, 81, 101, 119, 146, 149; payers or purchasers of 25,40; prices or inflation 63-4, 91, 103, 148; providers, professionals, or provision of 19, 40, 49, 56, 61, 63, 71, 73-4, 76-8, 82, 95, 98, 101-4, 134, 149-50,162-4, 166; programs 67, 93, 156; options 151; organizations, facilities, or enterprises 56, 71, 74, 78, 88, 101, 105, 113, 121-3, 134, 166; rationing 118; reform 10-11, 21, 29, 32-3, 88, 104, 133, 137-8, 148, 155, 157, 165, 167; regulation 33,91; savings 150, 162-3; services and treatment regimes 64, 67, 69-71, 78, 88-9, 92-3, 99-100, 102 109-10, 119-20, 131-2, 135, 137-8, 147-9, 151, 154, 163-4, 166; system 10, 15-6, 18, 20, 22, 24-5, 28, 33, 38, 40-2, 54, 60, 67, 74, 79, 81-2, 89, 93, 95, 98-100, 103-5, 108, 110, 113-4, 118-21, 123, 133, 135, 137-8, 154-5, 164, 167-8; utilization 55, 167
Health Care Financing Agency (HCFA) 72, 75, 91-2, 101, 104, 117, 122
Health entitlement 36, 53, 56, 143-6, 149-50, 155-7, 160-2, 165, 167-8, 172
Health insurance 9-11, 15, 18-21, 25-29, 31-4, 36-42, 44-52, 60, 64, 67-73, 75-80, 82-6, 88-96, 98-105, 107-8, 111-2, 114-20, 123-4, 126-8, 131-5, 137, 139-149, 151-4, 159-60, 162-8, 170-2
Health Maintenance Organization (HMO) 54, 61, 63, 69, 71, 73-4, 78, 85, 91, 122, 139
Health Savings Accounts (HSAs) 36, 38-41
Heffler, S. 34, 44-5, 87
Hiatt, H.H. 75, 84
Himmelstein, D.U. 76-80, 86-7, 100, 103, 109-10, 113, 124,157
Hoffman, C. 20, 44
Hospital: hospital admissions, stays, or visits 17-8, 22, 50, 56; hospital insurance or prepayment 27, 50, 52-3, 91; hospital medical staff or physicians' workshop 22, 50-52; hospital-physician sector or dominance 48-60, 62-3, 65-7, 102, 104, 106, 163; hospital technology 50-2; investor-owned hospitals versus not-for-profit 68;
House Ways and Means Committee 26-7
Hussy, P.S. 43

I

Ideology or ideological 32-4, 126, 132-3, 135-7, 142, 146, 148-52, 165
Ifill, G. 31, 44

Incentives: 82, 113-4, 148, 151; for Health Savings Accounts 38, 40; for consumer values 72, 105, 109; for economic growth 88; for over-utilization 113; for quality 24; for special care programs 71, 73

Income-related catastrophic health insurance coverage 36-7, 47, 68-9, 71, 76, 103-4, 116-7, 121-3, 133-7, 139, 142-45, 148-9 152, 154, 159-60, 163, 166, 170, 172

Institute of Medicine 24

Internal Revenue Service 90

J

Japan 16-18

Johnson, H. 30-1, 44

Johnson, President Lyndon 27, 32

K

Kaiser Family Foundation 142, 148, 153

Keeham, S. 44

Kennedy, Senator Edward 28, 77, 140

Kiley, T. 43

Kim, M. 43

King County Medical Society 52

Krauss, C. 120, 124

L

Labor unions 129, 136, 148

Lazenby, H.C. 54, 84-5, 169

Letsch, S.W. 54, 84-5

Levit, K.R. 54, 62, 84-5, 162, 169

Liberals 28, 32-4, 38, 126, 141-3, 145-6, 149-50, 152, 168

Lillie-Blanton, M. 20, 44

Lipsitz, S. R. 43

Long, A.M. 85

Long, Senator Russell 140

Longman, P. 67, 85, 105, 124

Low dollar coverage or benefits-see first-dollar coverage or benefits

Luft, H.S. 57, 68, 86

M

Managed care organizations, plans, or programs 48-50, 61-64, 76, 99, 139, 141, 149-50, 155, 162-3, 166

Manning, W.G. 60, 85

Market-driven system or health care reform 41-2, 46-7, 68-9, 82, 97-100, 104-5, 110, 112, 114, 122, 165

Martin, 84, 169

Marttila, J. 43

Massachusetts Universal Health Insurance legislation 9, 11, 144, 151

Matsumoto, M.F. 87

McDonnell, P.A. 85

McKusick, D.R. 87

Medicaid 19, 27-8, 34, 54, 87, 91, 95, 116, 145, 150-1, 155-6, 158

Medicare 19, 27-8, 32-8, 46, 53-54, 56, 58, 62-3, 79-80, 85, 87, 89-90, 93, 95-6, 99, 116, 119-20, 128, 133, 136, 138, 140, 144-5, 148, 150, 153, 155-62, 165, 167-8, 170-2

Mills, Chairman Wilbur 27-8

Monheit, A.C. 20, 43

Monopolization, price fixing, collusion 48, 106-8, 110,

Monopsony market 111

Moral hazard 69, 72, 102 163

Mullins, B. 133, 153

N

National Association of Manufacturers 31

National Health Board 91-2

National health insurance (NHI) 11, 15, 18, 26, 33-4, 38, 45-6, 76-8, 80-1, 83-4, 86, 93-4, 96, 111, 118-9, 123, 126, 133, 135, 142, 152, 165-7

National Health Insurance Act (USNHI) 77-80, 83, 93, 95-6

National Program Advisory Board 79

Newhouse, J.P. 54, 56, 64, 69, 85-6, 123-4

New Zealand 22

Nixon, President Richard 34, 126, 140

O

Olin, G.L. 85

Olson, M. 106-8, 124

Rose, H. 153
Rosenberg, N. 105, 125